It pays to
be kind.

It pays to be kind.

How I built a billion-dollar company treating people right.

Sig Anderman

A

FIRST EDITION

ISBN 9798989101207 | ISBN 9798989101214(ebook)

Printed in the United States of America

Designed by Heather Scott/Informal Practice

To my late wife Susan, whose unconditional love
and support made our life together—the lowest
lows and the greatest highs—truly spectacular.
Her kindness continues to teach me.

Contents

It pays to
be kind.

The Power of Kindness

It was 9:25 a.m. on April 15, 2011, and twenty-five of us were stepping, single file, up a narrow circular stairwell behind the scenes of the New York Stock Exchange. My palms were sweating and I could feel tears prickling the corners of my eyes. I was flanked by people I loved: My Ellie Mae co-founder and colleagues, my wife Susan, our children, even our grandchildren, ranging in age from 5 to 11. I had insisted that every single person was essential.

"Too many people!" the Exchange had warned. "This is for business associates only." But there was no way I was arriving at this moment in my life—ringing the bell on the floor of the New York Stock Exchange at age 70 to celebrate my fourth, last, and most successful business venture going public at a $140 million valuation—without every one of them by my side. This was their story as much as it was mine, and none of our successes had ever been guaranteed.

Emerging from the staircase to the platform was breathtaking. Lights and cameras came into focus, as did the stock ticker tape above us projecting ELLI: Ellie Mae's newly minted symbol. My heart rate spiked. Just forty-eight hours earlier, we were uncertain the company had enough support to go public at all. A decade ago, my wife and I had been sitting in the office of a bankruptcy lawyer.

The years in between were rocky. I willed myself to take in the moment, and those tears stinging my eyes now streamed down my cheeks. I took the hands of the people on either side of me: Susan and my 11 year-old grandson, Simon.

This was the culmination of forty years of relentless work, collaboration, and good luck. It was a once-in-a-lifetime success that grew from the foundation of the simplest and most important business principle I know: kindness.

This is a book about how kindness worked for me—and how it can work for you. It's the story of how being kind, combined with simple, unremarkable traits we are all born with, took me from a poor, tough neighborhood in New York—with parents who never went to college and struggled to earn a barely subsistence living—to building a wildly successful, multi-billion-dollar business, a storybook marriage, and a family life overflowing with love.

My formula for success is likely different from what you've read before. It doesn't require special training, degrees, or preternatural brilliance, let alone the seemingly superhuman business skills of America's corporate giants. Instead, I believe success requires inherent traits we all can master: compassion, perseverance, hard work, and a willingness to take chances and seize opportunities. At the front line of those lessons is the most important one: **the power of kindness.**

Mind you, kind doesn't mean being soft or a pushover. **Being kind means being considerate and thoughtful and caring about others, while still being determined and goal driven. Kindness and strength can go hand in hand. It can just mean being yourself, kind and empathetic, but still decisive and confident. Kindness works because it stands out. It sets you apart.** It's a winning strategy in business and in life.

By nature, I was kind to people for as long as I can remember. Even in kindergarten, I shared my sandbox and got the "Outstanding" grade for "Works and Plays Well with Others." Maybe it was because I wasn't big enough or tough enough to get my way through brute force. But for whatever reason, I was a kind kid from the very beginning.

Over the years, my kindness gene matured into a powerful force to achieve success and happiness. Along the way, I learned that being kind is its own variety of superpower. It means listening to others and really paying attention. Being considerate of others' needs and taking a step back to try to see a challenge or opportunity from someone else's frame of reference is a valuable tool. Tuning into an empathetic understanding of how another person feels in a given situation can be a life-changer.

Showing kindness does not mean settling for less, no matter how the world has tried to spin it that way. If we look at some of the world's most famous celebrities, we can see that being genuinely kind worked in their favor.

Steph Curry, who leads our local basketball team, the Golden State Warriors, exudes kindness towards his teammates on the court, and with community initiatives like the Eat. Learn. Play. Foundation—all while winning four NBA championships in eight years. Dolly Parton and Willie Nelson are both wildly successful public figures who are as famous for the ways they support their families, hometowns, and the causes they champion as they are for their music. Wayne Gretzky, the greatest hockey player ever, is known for emulating the qualities he learned from his late father: "Money didn't really matter to him; friendships did. Hard work mattered to him. Being passionate, being unselfish." And Don Nelson—Hall of Fame-honored Boston Celtics basketball player, second winningest coach in NBA history, and one of the toughest competitors in the sport—prioritized kindness after the 2023 fires on Maui by donating all his rental properties on island to displaced folks.

But in day-to-day life, and in the realm of business—especially among risk-taking entrepreneurs and high-profile politicians—*compassion*, *kindness*, and *empathy* are not words one often hears. These attributes are frequently dismissed, downgraded, smeared, mocked, and debased. It's no coincidence that these qualities are also stereotypically assigned to women, who make up a meager 10% of the CEOs on this year's Fortune 500 list—and that's an all-time high.

The world defines success by finances and popularity. Many people assume that those who reach the top are predominantly self-centered schemers, and perhaps there are some people who fit that bill. Unfortunately, the mean and lurid often dominate the headlines—the latest billionaire to deny basic rights to his workers or the newest breed of grinning swindler to separate people from their money. But self-interest isn't a universal characteristic of truly successful people. The people who fill the headlines may have money in the bank, but they do not have what I believe to be the quintessential characteristics of the most successful people in the world. But it's the garbage that gets the clicks. The worst in us tends to get the most attention. This is a pattern we must change.

Regrettably, the media's obsession with promoting the nasty and selfish extends beyond celebrity and business and into politics. Rude behavior, bigoted speech, and abject insults from so-called leaders have tricked many into thinking that crudeness and cruelty are direct pathways to power and wealth. Too many go along with this notion, that those who are greedy, selfish, and abrasive are more successful or more effective than people who aren't. But I believe being a jerk is overrated when it comes to all measures of success. The crudely selfish approach has been front and center, and the opposing force—kindness—has devolved into an undervalued commodity.

How can the genie be stuffed back into the bottle? How can the nasty factor in American public life and American culture be dialed back? How can *kindness, compassion,* and *selflessness* make a comeback—and be honored as indispensable qualities of a successful person, essential components of being a good citizen in a democracy?

The short answer is: We can do it—one person at a time. It's not that kind people aren't out there. They are. The world is overflowing with kind people. We're everywhere, but we're often overshadowed. Very few people hear about it when somebody does something nice. And that's not just because of nastiness in the media, business, and politics—it's a challenging time to be alive, period.

I consider myself part of a very privileged demographic and era: being born white and male in mid-twentieth century America gave me opportunities that would be unheard of at any other time. I wasn't buying my first home or seeking my first job in the midst of a financial or climate crisis, and zillionaires of the kind there are now just didn't exist back then. Putting aside the undeniable hurdles of anti-semitism my family faced as Jewish immigrants, I'm well aware that I occupy a highly advantageous spot in the world. I also know that what I do with that privilege matters, and for me, that begins with being kind—and doing my best to spread kindness in the world.

Kindness is always within reach. Anyone, at any time, can be kind. You may never slam dunk a basketball like some of the best athletes on the planet. You may never sing like Andrea Bocelli, or become the second coming of Einstein. But kind? Kind you can do. Right now, tomorrow, and next week. And not only does kindness feel good, it's also a legitimate path to success.

The truth is, it *pays* to be *kind,* and in this book, I'm going to show you how that's possible. Along with learning about the powers of perseverance, personal connection and fate, contributing to society, surrounding yourself with an A-Team, and following other healthy business practices, in this book, you'll learn that being kind is foundational to true success. (Look out for key lessons in **bold text** throughout the book, revisited in my Tips for Startup Success at the end.)

I'm going to explore the qualities that comprise kindness, demonstrate compassion, and work with others to amplify the presence and power of kindness in society. It's time for each of us to become ambassadors of kindness. I'm hoping the story I tell in this book will inspire you and others to put more into being kind, and that this objective will grow into a larger movement.

We've seen plenty of pessimism and despair. I'm going to stick with optimism and urge others to do the same. Why not believe that with a little effort, kindness can make a comeback? Maybe it's a conversation we can all have together.

Wouldn't that be nice?

Nice Guys Don't Finish Last: Where Kindness Can Take You

I Had the Time of My Life in a Catskills Resort

Growing up in New York in the 1940s and '50s, I survived by being kind. I was a quick study, and my parents bounced me not one but two grades forward. I was already small for my age, and being younger than my classmates by two whole years, I was always the smallest boy in my class. Good thing I was nice, day after day. This was no act. I was just doing what came naturally, but it worked out for me: Being kind earned me friends and protection. I had to constantly watch for little gangs of boys who might be of a mind to push me around—or a lot worse.

My family lived on West 16th Street in Manhattan, straddling Hell's Kitchen and Chelsea. Though my family was Jewish, most of the kids on our block were Irish. The next block west was home to a Puerto Rican community. The streets were filled with tough guys of all ethnic backgrounds, but as it turned out, kids weren't inclined to pick fights with me. One of my best pals was Jo Jo Flores, a year or two older than me, a foot taller, and tough as nails—opposites do tend to attract. No one picked a fight with Jo Jo, who was Puerto Rican, or with any of his friends. Jo Jo used to walk with me to my violin lessons after school, and his mere presence offered protection against the kids who would otherwise heckle me on the way. Let's be honest: In New York, "kind" was not always a compliment.

I was four years old in July 1946 when play-by-play announcer Red Barber gave Brooklyn Dodgers manager Leo "The Lip" Durocher a hard time one day at the Polo Grounds.

"Why don't you be a nice guy for a change?" Barber asked Durocher.

The manager was stung.

"A nice guy?! A nice guy!?" he shouted. "I never saw a nice guy who was any good when you needed him. … I'll take the guys who aren't nice. The guys who would put you in a cement mixer if they felt like it."

Durocher pointed over to the New York Giants dugout and toward their manager, Mel Ott.

"Look over there," he said. "Do you know a nicer guy than Mel Ott? Or any of the other Giants? Why, they're the nicest guys in the world! And where are they? In last place!"

Of those words, the expression "Nice guys finish last" was born, and believe me, I heard that a lot when I was a kid growing up on 16th Street. But I never cared about any of that. **I just had to be myself, which meant being nice to people, not just on my good days but on all my days. Kindness came naturally to me, as I had learned it early on from my parents.**

I was born in New York in September 1941, three months before the bombing at Pearl Harbor. Our apartment on West 16th was in a grimy, industrial part of the city, with a mixture of tenement-like walk-up buildings (like the one we lived in), some newer modern elevator apartment buildings, and manufacturing plants. Right across the street from our apartment was a coal-burning Con Edison power plant, with a textile factory next door. The streets, and the inside of our apartment, were always covered with the soot of the power plant and the furnaces burning coal in the older buildings.

When the huge London Terrace apartment complex on nearby West 23rd Street opened in 1930, the *Brooklyn Eagle* hailed it as "the largest single residential development on record," with 2,000 individual apartments. It was a beautiful complex. To me, it was the height of fancy. Even beyond fancy. It was glamorous. After all, my family—my parents, two sisters, and, for a long time, my mother's youngest brother Manny and my grandma Esther—all lived in a three bedroom, one bathroom walk-up apartment. Our rent was $45 a month.

My father, Simon, came to the United States with his family in 1913 when he was five years old from what was then Austria—present-day Ukraine. His father had died by that time, and his mother, Esther, decided she wanted a better life for her family, so she made the move. How's that for courage? She arrived in New York with four kids, no husband, and five dollars. Not even a cell phone! My gratitude for her bravery has often made me wonder about the impulse that drove her.

Back home in Buchach, in a region along the Strypa River that was then part of the Austro-Hungarian Empire, my grandmother and her family had a lot more than five dollars—in fact, they lived a quite comfortable life. According to my Aunt Sarah, grandma's oldest child and ten years my father's elder, my grandfather Alexander Zisha Anderman was a cattle merchant, and the family in Buchach lived stably and well. A majority of the large Jewish population of Buchach would be slaughtered by the Nazis and their Ukrainian collaborators in 1944. But in 1913, the terrible anti-Semitism of later years had not yet taken hold.

How lucky I am, and how lucky my family is, that my

grandmother had the fortitude, the foresight, and the selflessness to make that move. Not for herself, but for her children, for me and her other grandchildren, and for all her descendents. Manhattan was no Buchach, but it was a place of future promise for our family, particularly as our Jewish relatives in Ukraine faced certain death during World War II.

I worked alongside my father from the time I was ten years old, helping out at the dry-cleaning store he ran on 7th Avenue and 13th Street, a few blocks from our apartment. My parents' work ethic was endless, and they held supreme one cardinal rule: *Don't get into debt.* My father never took up a credit card or a mortgage, and his mantra became my own. Earning a paycheck meant I didn't have to rely on my parents for spending money, which they didn't have much of in the first place. Plus, I didn't want them asking me what I was going to do with it.

My first paid role at the shop was delivering cleaned clothes to customers. I would pile five or six deliveries over my shoulder, my fingers grasping the wire hangers as I made my rounds through Greenwich Village and Chelsea. I can still feel the pinch of the wire hangers digging into my fingers. Relief came slowly as I dropped off my deliveries. By the time I got back to the cleaning store, just as the swelling in my fingers went down, I was ready to deliver another five or six batches of newly cleaned and pressed clothing.

The tradeoff was worth it: A little bit of pain for the freedom of spending money to buy my own lunch—and occasionally some First Day Covers at the local stamp shop. I knew one day the work would pay off; after all, by 1947, while barely earning enough to live on, my parents had saved up $1500 to buy a small summer cottage on two acres, forty miles north of New York.

At P.S. 3, my junior high school in west Greenwich Village, I learned, like all boys do, about the limits of being nice. It might help you get the girl—but it's not enough to keep her. Having skipped fourth grade and one year of junior high, I was eleven years old in ninth grade, surrounded by fourteen and fifteen year-olds.

I'll never know how I worked up the courage to ask, or why she said yes, but for the ninth-grade prom I decided to ask Dolores Sarubbi, who was a real knockout. Dolores was not only very pretty and very developed—she was "stacked," as we put it at the time— she was also two years older than me, and could have passed for ten. I was a skinny kid with this total bombshell.

I imagine Dolores accepted my invitation to the dance out of the sheer kindness of her heart, and we mixed it up on the dance floor a time or two—my older cousin Cecile had taught me how to do the Lindy hop. But I didn't quite have the self confidence to try to kiss Dolores that night. I think she had other things in mind, anyway, as she left with some other guy. Being with me must have felt to her like escorting her baby brother around. I took the subway home alone that night. So much for being nice.

Six years later, the *Brooklyn Daily* published an anecdote about Dolores that caught my eye: In a February 1962 "Magic Carpet Over Broadway" column, Joe Califf quipped, "Dolores Sarubbi, the glamorous dark-eyed Village model, is slated for a Broadway show in the near future. With her face and body, Dolores is a sure bet for Hollywood." I always had good taste!

One weekend just after I started high school, my parents piled all five of us into the car as moving vans pulled up to our apartment on West 16th. They announced that we were moving out of the city. I was thirteen years old, and my whole life up to that day had been centered around a square block or two in the bustling heart of New York City. The cacophony of honking yellow taxis, buses belching diesel fumes, and police sirens echoing down broad avenues was the comfort of home.

Now, my parents announced, we were moving fifty miles north to Spring Valley, a summer resort area in the Ramapo Mountains. Spring Valley was fifty miles south of the Catskills, where they had bought a ramshackle farmhouse on ten acres a few years earlier—at $10,000, the property was quite an upgrade from their first purchase decades before. To be clear, this wasn't charming ramshackle, it was true ramshackle. Spring Valley was near the Hudson River, but it was across the river from fancier Westchester commuter towns like Scarsdale, Tarrytown, and Irvington. It was rural, and most of the ten acres that my parents bought were still wooded. Right across from our house, at that time, was Harm's Farm, a large dairy with a hundred acres of cows lowing day and night.

The move up the Hudson Valley meant that I'd be going to Spring Valley High School with my cousin David, who was a year behind me in school, even though he was a year and a half older. David and I grew up like brothers. We often slept in the same crib and played in the same playpen together. We always got along great, even though we were totally different. David was bigger than me, and strong and handsome. He was impulsive, confident, even impetuous. Always hard to control. I was thoughtful, pretty shy, and low-key to a fault.

I was the good little boy who played by the rules, while David refined his bad-boy persona. "While Sig was out practicing the violin, I was out stealing hubcaps," David remembers. "Even when we were little kids, Sig never made snap judgments. He was always the voice of reason. He always wanted to do the right thing."

By the time we hit puberty, David was running after girls and playing baseball and football. He was a popular guy, although a *White Plains Journal News* article would later report that he "was always in trouble at school and kicked off both the basketball and baseball teams for fooling around." When it was his turn to graduate, he was voted "Teacher's Torment" by his fellow graduating seniors. Under his yearbook picture, the caption mentioned his "flirtatious ways" and called him a "good looker."

Though I was two grades ahead and aced most of my classes, I watched David's confident social moves with amazement. He was my mentor in all the adult things I needed to learn—like girls. And sex. I got quite the education, covering subject matter my parents never dared to mention.

I was lucky to have David as a pal, along with his half-brother, David Sauberman. Their mother, my Aunt Frieda, had remarried. Her husband Lou Sauberman owned the Capri Hotel in our town of Spring Valley, which was part of an area called the mini-Borscht Belt—named for the thriving Jewish community that summered in resorts there each year.

If you've ever seen the movie *Dirty Dancing* with Patrick Swayze and Jennifer Grey, you've had a glimpse into the world of Jewish summer life in the Spring Valley summer resorts. The film was set in the early 1960s, just a few years after I started working at the Capri. When Patrick Swayze's working-class character tells another boy, "You just put your pickle on everybody's plate, college boy, and leave the hard stuff to me," it made me feel like I was back in the dining hall of the Capri, laying out pickles myself.

I loved the Capri. Young families with a couple of kids would come up from the city and spend anywhere from a few weeks to an entire summer there. The resort provided three meals a day, entertainment every night, a bar, and a swimming pool—everything you could dream of in a summer getaway. There was even a dance instructor! (Though he was no Swayze.)

I started out as a busboy in the children's dining room, which was the very lowest rung on the Capri's hierarchy of employment. I didn't make much, maybe a dollar per week per kid served. There would be one or two busboys for seventy-five kids, and my job was to run around trying to stop food fights or whatever else they were up to. I ran back and forth to the kitchen and cleaned up after them the whole time. Kids would ask for ice cream in the middle of breakfast, or pancakes for dinner, and we were obliged to comply. Summer by summer, I put in the time to work my way up the ranks—from children's busboy to children's waiter to main dining room busboy and then finally main dining room waiter.

In the summer of 1956, I met my first love at the Capri. Renee Posner was fourteen, one year younger than me, and she, her mother, her twin sister, and her brother were all guests at the hotel. Renee's father had died a few years before, and the hotel was a supportive community for the grieving family—though, at the time, I didn't appreciate how traumatic it was to lose a father at that young age. Our romance lasted for the summer and a month or two into the fall, after Renee and her family returned to the Bronx.

I quickly found a new girlfriend in high school. Julie Sarafan was a year or two older than me. She was very pretty and she could drive at night, both major benefits since at fifteen, I wasn't yet allowed to drive after dark. If we wanted to go on a date, Julie would drive us in her Plymouth, a wonderful car that had buttons that you pressed to put it in gear. We'd drive over to Perruna's in Spring Valley or up to Bear Mountain or to watch the "submarine races" along the Hudson River at our favorite "necking" spot. We had a great love affair.

By 1958, when I was sixteen, David and I decided it was time we awarded ourselves a plum summer gig at the Capri: We ran the snack bar at the swimming pool, and had a blast doing it. In those days, Coca-Cola would make up a sign for you, stamped out of aluminum, with the famous cursive "Coca-Cola" lettering accompanied by an image of the iconic glass bottle of Coke. I wish I had saved our sign: "Sig & Dave's."

David and I were two of probably forty boys and young men who worked that summer as waiters, busboys, lifeguards, and bellhops, whereas there were maybe ten or twelve girls our age employed there, usually as day camp counselors for the young children. A lot of the waiters were already quite grown up, often college and graduate school students who had worked at the Capri for years. It was an ideal job for guys working their way through dental school, medical school, or law school——a great way to sock away $200 or $300 a week without paying taxes, since it was all tips.

Every summer felt like a big reunion. We worked from the Fourth of July straight through to Labor Day without a single day off—child labor laws didn't exist then, much to the hotel owners' benefit. When I worked in the dining room, my day started at six-thirty or seven in the morning and went to nine at night, with a couple of breaks before and after the lunch rush. At night we'd all go out and party or play cards. It was crazy, crazy fun.

Like all the resorts, my aunt's hotel had a full-time band every summer, a piano player, a drummer, a bass player, and a clarinetist or saxophonist. The piano player in the summer of 1958 was a guy named Paul Kosarin who had just gotten married, right after his graduation from dental school. Paul was planning to report for duty in the Air Force that fall, but during the summer he was the piano player in the Capri Hotel's band. His wife, Donna, was hired as an "office girl."

One weekend, Paul's mother, father, and younger sister, Susan, came up to the resort to visit. Donna asked her new sister-in-law if she wanted to work with her in the office that summer.

"No thanks," Susan said. "I'd rather be in New York with my friends."

"What are you, crazy?" Her parents tried to dissuade her. "The Capri's got a swimming pool and tennis and a bunch of young people to hang out with—there's not much going on at home in the Bronx."

But Susan was resolute. She and her parents said their good-byes and began the long drive back to New York. Somewhere along the way, though, as she gazed out the window at the beauty of the countryside, Susan had a change of heart. Her parents gladly turned the car around and she decided to give working life at the Capri a try. Susan started in the office that same day, wearing her sister-in-law's clothing until her parents could return with some fresh outfits.

As it turned out, that U-turn the Kosarins made was a life-changer for me.

It's hard to overstate the electricity that surged through the Capri when word spread—like wildfire—that there was a new office girl. As I said, the staff was overwhelmingly male, and they were extremely eager. Within hours of Susan starting work, there was a line of suitors out the door, a queue of hunky, young profession-als and students just hovering around the front office, hoping for a chance to talk to her.

Did I mention that Susan was absolutely gorgeous? Sixteen, with a body that never ended. I was spellbound. She was the most beautiful girl I'd ever seen. But I was in the background, watching from a distance, as all these mature young men were hitting on her, and I was this skinny kid, not yet seventeen. I presumed that I had no shot. All I could think was: "How the hell could I ever get through to her with all this noise?" I was just graduating high school, and all the other guys seemed way more impressive and worldly. So I turned to the one strength I knew I could always count on: Being kind.

I thought about all the people in my life I'd grown close to by being nice, all the times I'd turned around intimidating situations by flexing kindness. It was time for me to summon my cousin David's confidence and talk to the most beautiful girl I'd ever met. I knew that if I could just become Susan's friend, her trusted confidant, I wouldn't have to worry about being eclipsed by the older guys wooing her.

Every day, I looked for an excuse to swing by the office, ask her how she was doing, make a little small talk, and try to move on before I made a pest of myself. (Or got run over by the stampede of guys all there to talk to her as well.)

Day by day, I worked up my courage practicing with David, and finally asked Susan if I could take her out for a drive. She said yes. I was elated.

There was only one problem: My car. I loved my 1951 green Plymouth Cranbrook sedan, but it had come cheap—free, actually—and for good reason: There were a few holes in the floorboards, which was really just a metal pan that had rusted out. My uncle had given me the car after he drove it 100,000 miles. In those years, driving an American car 100,000 miles was a miracle.

As Susan and I drove around near Spring Valley that first time, cruising along the long finger of DeForest Lake near the Hudson River, I tried not to make it obvious that I noticed Susan noticing the holes. How could she not? She could see the road passing by underneath! We stopped at the Plaza Diner in Spring Valley and shared a tuna sandwich on rye toast, her favorite. I didn't really like tuna, but I wanted to be nice.

Through it all, we talked and talked and talked. Actually, Susan did most of the talking. I was a good listener. I loved talking to her. But I didn't love all the topics we covered. Even though I felt like

I was on a date, Susan didn't see it that way. She would tell me all about her old boyfriends and about the big crush she had on David, my cousin. I understood the appeal, even though it drove me crazy to hear it from the girl I had a crush on. (David, now a handsome man in his eighties, has been married eight times—one of the all-time great romancers.)

As the weeks passed, though, Susan's and my conversations grew deeper. I got her. I was understanding, and kind. **I learned how to listen and be compassionate and empathetic.** The more we talked, the more we really started to like each other. Well, I had liked her from the second I saw her, but soon she started to like me, too. Sure enough, I had become her confidant and friend. And then, just like that, we were going out.

From our very first kiss standing next to the green cigarette machine at the back of the "nightclub" in the main building of the Capri, it was electric. There was a kinetic energy between us, with all those hormones raging, and so many opportunities to have fun together. Everything that summer—actually, every summer at the Capri— was condensed. Working at the resort for two and a half months without a day off, together all the time for so many hours a day, it felt like spending a year together. We became very close very quickly, and all the other guys were jealous that little Siggy ended up with gorgeous Susan.

The nice guy had finally finished first.

CHAPTER 2

Hope Through Kindness: Making a Difference in Young People's Lives

The whole time my kids were growing up, I would always tell them, "Listen, you have to study harder than everyone else and get all A's." My parents had drummed that into me and my sisters daily as we grew up. They reached adulthood in the mid-1930s in New York, during the Great Depression. I am sure the possibility of another depression, with millions out of work and jobs hard to come by, was always on their mind. On top of that, anti-semitism was prevalent while they were growing up—even in the United States. Many employers—including most banks, insurance companies, and law firms—wouldn't hire Jews. This meant that for the relatively fewer jobs that were available to them, they had to work harder and perform better than the rest. So my parents' loving academic demands were actually intended to help us overcome discrimination. A valuable lesson.

Years later, when my children were long since out of school, they came across my actual City College transcript and were flabbergasted at what they saw. "Dad, you've got to be kidding! This is your college transcript?" Let's just say I did not get all A's.

Even though I lived some fifty miles away, I went to City College in Manhattan. My parents weren't very sophisticated about planning for higher education—neither they nor anyone in their family or social circle had ever gone to college. And they didn't have the money for tuition, anyway. City College was free. So, City College it was.

It was 1959, I was commuting to college, living at home with my parents in Spring Valley, and I was always exhausted. Every morning I would get up at six o'clock and drive to the bus stop in town, which was about ten miles away. I would park, wait for the Red and Tan Lines bus, get on the bus, and ride for an hour and a half from Spring Valley to the Port Authority Building in Manhattan on 181st Street, stopping at a dozen small towns along the way. From there, I would take the subway to 138th Street in Manhattan, walk a few blocks to City College, go to four or five hours of classes, and finally, after classes finished, do the reverse all over again. I'd get home at eight or nine o'clock at night—or even later if I did anything social after class, which was rare.

I had the constant feeling that I just wanted to curl up somewhere and go to sleep. One morning, being so exhausted, I was slow to react when a car driving in front of me on Route 45 slammed on its brakes at a red light. Boom! I smashed into the back of the car and ruined the front end of my beloved Plymouth. It was crushed, and so was I.

Being without a car or any money to spare, I had to get that car fixed, and fast. Walter Stansbury, a handyman my folks had living on our property in exchange for occasional work, offered to help.

"Let's fix it ourselves," he said.

We went to the junkyard, found two new fenders, a whole new

front, and a radiator to replace the one that got smashed into the engine block. I wasn't about to spend fifty bucks for a paint job; that was money I did not have, so I bought a can of green paint for six bucks and painted the car myself. I splurged to buy a can of silver paint for the bumpers. I loved that car, and restoring it gave me a boost of needed energy.

Back in my routine with my trusty Plymouth, I discovered another ritual that would become my favorite part of college: shooting pool with my friend Chris Singh. Chris and I were in the same history class, and we would often grab lunch and shoot pool for an hour between classes. We were evenly matched with a pool cue and would always bet on our games, a quarter or something, just to make it more exciting. One day I was racking the balls up for another game, and Chris told me he wouldn't be seeing me for a few weeks.

"Law boards," he said. "I'm applying to law school and need to take the LSAT test."

The LSAT? I had no idea what law boards were, and had never heard of the LSAT. I'd never even met a lawyer, nor did my parents know any. I had, however, seen *Perry Mason*—in which Raymond Burr starred as a TV lawyer, and which was in its first seasons at the time. I was intrigued at the thought of someone I knew actually studying to become a lawyer. This was a strange, new concept to me.

I asked Chris some questions about the law boards, and he kept telling me how hard they were, notoriously difficult. The more he talked, the more I felt a growing twinkle in my eye. I may not have been sold on my math major, and I was not the best student—as my kids later discovered—but I had a knack for numbers and figuring out problems with logic. This meant I had a certain amount of skill in acing tests. Which was useful, since I could never seem to memorize details.

"Why don't we bet on it?" I challenged Chris.

"Wait, what?" He was, rightfully, confused.

"The law boards," I said. "I bet you twenty bucks I can beat you on the law boards. I'll take them, too."

Chris looked at me like I was crazy. He clearly thought I was going to lose. But twenty bucks was about enough to cover the exam fee and have some left over for a sandwich.

"How much are you going to study?" Chris asked as we shook on the bet.

"Study?" I grinned at him. Of course not. He shook his head, eager for the twenty bucks he was sure he'd be getting.

Two weeks later, I walked into the ballroom of a midtown Manhattan hotel with hundreds of other young men—in those days very few women had the opportunity to become lawyers. I went in stone cold, with no idea what to expect, and I aced the thing. My score was stratospheric, one of the top scores in the country. Soon after that, I started getting a lot of mail.

Law schools from around the nation were reaching out to me, asking if I would please consider applying to their fine academic institution. I'm talking about great law schools, like the University of Chicago and the University of Virginia. As the first few letters arrived, I tossed them in the trash. Law school? Who were they kidding? I was more interested in collecting my twenty bucks from Chris! But as more letters came in, I began to wonder if they knew something about me that I didn't yet know myself. Maybe I was going to law school.

Throughout this time, Susan and I were dating. She opened up many new worlds for me, starting with her great love of art and classical music, which became a lifetime passion of mine. Considering our deepening relationship, I was not about to move to Chicago or Charlottesville. California—and all points in between—were completely out of the question. I wanted to stay in New York, and I ended up applying and getting accepted to New York University Law School, which was thrilling.

There was only one problem: The tuition was $1,200 a year, which I didn't have. I'd have to come up with a bucket of money to pay for school. Actually, there were two problems: the law school required that I add some liberal arts classes before graduating. So I also had some coursework to make up.

To solve both problems, I decided to work as a school teacher. It was perfect: I could continue at City College from September to January to complete the remaining coursework, graduate, and then work full-time as a teacher from January to June and save up enough money for law school. New York City school teachers were being paid $100 a week, so in 20 weeks—half a year—I'd earn $2,000, enough for tuition with room to spare. I had never thought I would become a teacher, despite advice my parents had given me that teaching would be a great profession, with stability and a retirement plan—important for those who grew up during the Great Depression. But teaching just happened for me, and the experience had a lasting impact.

It showed me that sometimes being kind means knowing when it's time to be a little gruff, tough even. That was the advice I got from friends when I told them that to pay for law school, I was going to work from January to June as a teacher in P.S. 93, a South Bronx school that was known for being the educational home to some of the most difficult students in the city. P.S. 93, at the corner of Elder and Story Avenues, was a block away from the Bruckner Expressway in the Soundview neighborhood of the South Bronx, near where the Bronx Kill flows into the East River, across from Rikers Island. Rikers—as in, New York City's main prison complex. The class I was inheriting had, in fact, gone through three different teachers in the five months before they hired me.

It was such a tough job—teaching a fifth grade class of students who had been previously expelled from other schools—that I'm sure just about anybody who showed up would have been hired. The school was so eager to find a teacher that my get-acquainted session with the principal, Jack August, barely counted as a job interview. Jack was a kind man, tall, with a dark rim of hair around a bald head. Within five minutes, he hired me. I didn't look much older than the kids I would be teaching, and I certainly looked a lot less tough.

I'll never forget my first visit to the classroom at the end of December. Desks were overturned, books were torn and thrown all over the place. Thirty-two students had been running amok. I thought I'd stepped into a scene from the movie *Blackboard Jungle*, which came out a few years earlier, painting a challenging picture of a very similar school in the South Bronx. **I knew I needed to prepare myself, so I interviewed teachers at the model elementary school run by City College in Harlem. As I shared the challenge ahead with these teachers, they offered suggestions to guide my approach and behavior. And I got to work.**

Following advice from the teachers I spoke with and my own experiences growing up, I realized that what these kids needed was someone to show them that he truly cared whether they succeeded or failed in school. I knew that compassion, in this case, meant setting firm guidelines and providing structure that would demonstrate to these students that someone was actually interested in what they did each day. I also knew that I had to find a way to keep the classroom neat and tidy, or I would have no shot at enforcing any kind of order or decorum.

It took me hours, but I got the place whipped into shape, all ready for the first day of school in January. I set up the desks and the chairs, put all the books in order, and wrote all across the wall-to-wall blackboard at the front of the class. I spelled out my name, Mr. Anderman, and wrote down assignments and rules for the class. I made it clear that the rules were very important.

YOU HAVE TO SHOW UP ON TIME

YOU HAVE TO KEEP QUIET UNLESS YOU ARE CALLED UPON

YOU HAVE TO DO YOUR HOMEWORK

WHEN ASKED TO PARTICIPATE, YOU HAVE TO PARTICIPATE

In 1962, every school day began with all the kids in the schoolyard. They would mill around, talking in little groups, and when the whistle blew it was time for the students to get in line to enter their classroom. On my first day as the new teacher——not much older than a teenager—I heard the whistle and waited for my students to line up. And waited. And waited. Fortunately, I'd expected this.

I decided to use a technique someone had explained to me. The students were still milling around, but I did not say a word. I kept a stern look on my face and nudged them into line using hand gestures, one by one, still not speaking. The other classes had all lined up and marched upstairs to class, but there we were in the schoolyard, the only class left. I was still lining them up with this very stoic, expressionless face.

Finally, they were in line, and I was still silent. I motioned for them to follow me. Together we walked up to the third floor, the top floor of the school. Still not saying a word, I motioned for them to line up against the wall by the door. I pointed to the first kid. I had him come inside and sat him down in the first seat. Then I motioned to the second kid to come sit down, brought him in, and sat him down, still mute. Up on the board were the rules I had written out for them. In hindsight, I'm sure they all thought I was crazy.

Once I had walked four or five kids in, I was heading outside when I heard some noise in the classroom. I went back in and saw a kid talking. I walked right over to him and, with calm determination, careful not to touch him at all, I grabbed his collar. "Remember," I said, gesturing to the blackboard. "No talking until you're asked to say something."

Those were the first words I spoke to my new class of students.

"Do you understand that?" I went on.

He nodded his head, eyes wide. At this point, they knew I was crazy, unlike any other teacher they had ever encountered. They were just scared enough to take me seriously.

I was very, very strict. The boys had to wear a tie. I bought a bunch of ties for them using my first paycheck, so they had ties. They had to have a handkerchief, so I brought in a bunch of handkerchiefs. They had to have clean hands and look like they took their studies seriously. There was no Internet then to do instant research, but it turns out that kids who wear uniforms to school and who have strict rules do better and have a better experience. Over time, as students make the choice to invest themselves in their studies, you can relax those rules.

One of the rules I'd written out on the board was that the kids had to do their homework, and I had to show I meant it. The first week, when the very first kid showed up without his homework, I told him he had to leave.

"You didn't bring your homework in?" I asked this little kid. "OK, go home. Come back tomorrow—with your homework."

The little kid walked out of the classroom and started walking home, and I went back to teaching my kids. Mr. Fliegel, the assistant principal, came rushing into the room with a look of panic on his face.

"Did you see? Did you see?" he was shouting. "One of your kids is walking across Bruckner Boulevard!"

I remained cool.

"No, I didn't see, but that makes sense," I said. "I sent him home."

"You sent him *home*?" he said. "You can't *do* that!"

I kept my calm and walked out of the kids' hearing distance, so we could talk this over.

"Look, if you want me to teach, I have to teach," I said. "Nobody else has succeeded here. I'll make these kids great. I really will. But you have to let me try it my way."

I didn't have to remind him of all the other teachers who had quit between September and December. Surprisingly, Mr. Fliegel relented. I had to send another kid home for not doing homework that week. And the next week, another. But soon the message sunk in. They all showed up. They all wore their uniform. They all did their homework.

In fact, these kids did turn out to be great. They were simply off track because nobody had taken the time to understand them. The school system decided they were "bad kids" and disciplined them, but they never really invested in, cared for, got to know, or paid any attention to these students. **No one showed them kindness. Most of the teachers would yell at them, but I never yelled. I treated them like real people: I had real expectations for them, and real fondness.**

Over the next six months, I used kindness, discipline, and a bit of reverse psychology to move up their reading skills until they were at grade reading level, and even won some academic competitions. I made staying after school a privilege, not a punishment—they could only stay after school if they were good. A lot of them stayed after school for extra activities, like preparing for the Bronx Science Fair for elementary schools—which they ended up winning.

I loved those kids. I loved their parents. I loved making a

difference in so many lives, at a time when a good break was all many of these young people needed. They succeeded because, maybe for the first time in their school careers, a teacher was kind to them. An authority figure appreciated them for who they were and who they might be someday. Kindness made a difference.

After my debut as a public school teacher, it was time for summer break and then law school. Since the school was in the Bronx and Susan lived in the Bronx, I had a routine of teaching and then seeing her afterward. Those six months were so fulfilling that I was tempted to change my career again and go into teaching full-time. But I decided I wanted to give law school a try—I was curious if I'd like it.

I ended up loving law school. Of all the school experiences I had in my life, I relished only two: kindergarten and law school. Everything else in between was just stressful. But law school allowed me to refine my problem-solving skills through the case study and Socratic methods. Most of the early classes in contracts and torts were intriguing history lessons from 18th and 19th century England that used real-life events to demonstrate how the law evolved to address disputes and challenges on both personal and societal levels.

By the end of my second year of law school, Susan and I had married at the very place where we met—the Capri Hotel. The romance was dreamy, but my parents thought we were crazy: We were 22, living together in the NYU dorms, and neither of us had a job. Within a year, our first daughter Elissa was born. And though I was very proud to graduate from law school, it was near impossible to find work. Strapped for cash, we moved in with Susan's family in the Bronx.

This may have been the first time I felt depressed in my life: I had a fancy law degree, a beautiful wife, and a new baby, yet I spent my days anxiously typing up cover letters to law firms, taking the subway into Manhattan to throw my hat in the ring again and again. Something had to change, and fast.

CHAPTER 3

Passion, Literature & David Sive

It was just dumb luck. I could have ended up with a mentor who was a tax lawyer or one who specialized in filing the paperwork for liquor licenses. Instead, a chance encounter offered me a catbird seat in the modern environmental movement, working alongside one of the most influential environmental attorneys ever: David Sive. Sive's 2014 obituary in the New York Times memorialized him as the "Father of Environmental Law," and his efforts almost single-handedly paved the way for the environmental movement in the United States. Sive handled many early landmark cases at a time when I was fortunate enough to be his assistant. Not coincidentally, he was one of the most caring humans I have ever met.

My future found me one afternoon as I was passing Bryant Park in Manhattan, a year after graduating from NYU Law School. The school's placement officer rounded the corner of the park, and I was thrilled to see her. I had just quit my first job out of law school; it was a one-man firm, and I couldn't make enough to live on. A few hours later, when the NYU placement officer stopped me on 40th Street, she told me she might have something for me.

"You know, Sig, just this morning I got a request from Winer, Neuburger & Sive," she said. "It's a great law firm. Why don't you call them? I won't put the posting up till tomorrow."

I called as soon as I got home, and went in for an interview the next morning. I wore my only suit: three-piece, black, with a matching vest. Their offices were in the Chrysler Tower East Building on the northeast corner of 42nd Street and Third Avenue, and I was impressed from the moment I arrived. The one-man firm where I was working before had a dingy little office that belonged in a Charles Dickens novel. The Winer, Neuburger & Sive offices were spacious, clean, and well-lit, with a fully stocked legal library. The furniture was new—and it actually matched.

I couldn't believe the contrast. I had been working in an office that felt like a cluttered, oversized closet, and now I was interviewing for a job in a firm with spacious offices and a library I wanted to hide away in, just to run my fingers over the spines of all those law volumes. There was an entire set on New York state case law, one on federal law, and numerous other volumes. I was over the moon.

David Sive's secretary, Rose Devery, brought me into his office. "Call me David," he said. David was composed, soft-spoken, and clearly very intelligent, not flashy in any way but considerate and—yes—kind. I met the other partners, Ralph Neuburger and David Winer, who were both a little older, and they were also very impressive. These were smart people doing important work. That came through loud and clear.

Incredibly enough, I got the job. I would earn $135 a week as an associate, on the lowest rung on the ladder, which meant running down to state or federal court to file papers and pick up documents. It was all new to me, and I was eager to soak up as much as I could, so I took to asking the court clerks if there were any trials going on I should check out. It was a legal education far beyond what I'd learned in the classroom. One time I sat in court for a few hours watching F. Lee Bailey, probably the most famous lawyer in the country at that time. I was mesmerized.

Bailey was flamboyant and brilliant, a real showman. As one star-struck newspaper columnist, Bob Talbert of South Carolina, put it in 1967, Bailey was "the longest ball hitter in the lawyer league… the name that strikes panic and fear in the hearts of prosecutors… the cool, swinging, classy knight in legal armor, mounted on headlines, charging through the halls of justice cutting down dragons of injustice and clearing the accused…handsome as a Hollywood handout, electric as a neon billboard, and much, much shorter than Bigger-Than-Life people should be."

David Sive was a very different type of brilliant lawyer. He did not hit you over the head with his erudition or the force of his intellect. His approach was understated, but he had an amazing mind for detail and nuance. Born in Brooklyn, Sive developed a deep respect for nature young, often visiting the Catskills with his family. He graduated from Brooklyn College in 1943 and brought a volume of Walden with him when he was sent to Europe during World War II. He was discharged from the military in October 1945, his mind—and commitment to doing good—sharp as ever.

Leaving the army, Sive went to law school, and soon became one of the foremost lawyers in the country. Working with him, I would need to go over briefs several times before I really understood them; Sive needed just one quick look, and he would have it down pat. In those days, we had no personal computers, and everything had to be typed out, so every attorney, including me, had a legal secretary. Sive could dictate an entire brief in one go and it would be perfect. You wouldn't have to make any corrections. You wouldn't have to adjust any punctuation or edit it in any way. It was just brilliant.

I saw what Sive could do and it boggled my mind. I should be so lucky. For me, dictating a brief was a painstaking process of start and restart, draft and redraft. I felt bad for my legal secretary, Barbara Holtz, to whom I would dictate what I wanted typed. She wrote it all down on a stenographer's pad, using special shorthand symbols, and then—incredibly—transcribed and typed it when she got back to her desk. All the typing was done manually. And for copies, she used carbon paper, those ink-coated sheets of blue paper placed between the sheets of white typing paper. In fact, the big technical innovation in my first couple years in practice was the introduction of carbon "sets," white sheets of typing paper interspersed with carbon paper and held together with glue at the very top. Copy machines wouldn't arrive for another few years. And word processors were twenty years away!

The first trip I made with the firm was to fly down to Washington in a DC-3, the old prop plane, and hole up at the Library of Congress to do research for Sive. What was I researching? The nature of beauty.

Sive put me to work helping him on a landmark environmental case involving a proposed Con Edison project to carve out part of a mountain along the Hudson River about sixty miles north of New York City, to build an elaborate hydroelectric plant. The case was Scenic Hudson Preservation Conference v. Federal Power Commission, but everyone referred to it as the Storm King Mountain case, using a name coined by a 19th-century writer for the dramatic, massive rock formation. It rose 1,300 feet straight up out of the Hudson River, looking much like El Capitan in Yosemite National Park in California. Colonial settlers gave it a less glamorous name—Butter Hill.

Our client, the Scenic Hudson Preservation Conference, was launched in 1963 by a small citizens group enraged—as *Hudson Valley Magazine* later explained it—when "Con Ed published a drawing of the proposed new plant: It showed the entire side of the mountain blown off. If these plans were approved as proposed, the Hudson Highlands landscape—renowned for its natural beauty and historical significance—would be irrevocably altered." Among the local residents backing the effort were Robert Boyle, a writer for *Sports Illustrated*, and prominent attorneys Leo Rothschild and Stephen Duggan. The cause drew widespread attention and thousands of donations were sent in from all over the country.

Though the Con Edison development would disrupt the striped bass population of the river and have a far-reaching environmental impact, our argument against it was also based on the central claim that the project would destroy this natural treasure of a beautiful, imposing mountain. As I conducted my research in Washington, I realized that defining "beauty" for the court was a tall challenge—especially when it applied to a mountain. I got nowhere at the Library of Congress. This wasn't an actress we were talking about. The only truth that emerged from my research was: *Beauty is in the eyes of the beholder.*

Top lawyers gravitated to the cause. They wanted to work with Sive, who they saw as a brilliant leader paving new ground. Of course, nobody knew where the case would lead. In hindsight, they hitched their wagon to the right force of nature.

I learned right away that Sive was an out-of-the-box thinker. One of his strengths was an ability to perceive and define beauty in a way the rest of us just couldn't. In 1970, he testified before the House Committee on Education and Labor and was introduced by Congressman Jim Scheuer of New York as, "perhaps the founder of the environmental law movement as we know it." Sive declared before the committee, "We must change the ways people look at the land and the manner in which they live. We must somehow convince people that roadsides and campgrounds and city streets are to be treated as their own living rooms."

This is where Sive's brilliance truly shined. He proceeded to quote from Thoreau, in Walden: "Most of the luxuries, and many of the so-called comforts of life, are not only not indispensable but positive hindrances to the elevation of mankind."

It was an emotional testimony at times, as when he said, "If our nation is one which is blessed with the greatest of resources and the greatest of natural wonders and the greatest areas of natural beauty, from…the Adirondack wilderness to the Grand Canyon and the Smokey and Cascade Mountains, then certainly we have, I think, some higher duty to fashion some kind of ethic, some kind of principle by which we treat this land with these resources and combine that with the technical advancement and technical knowledge we have."

In 1965, the Second Court of Appeals issued a dramatic ruling in the case, opening up the entire field of environmental law by finding that aesthetic concerns and regard for the environment provided enough legal basis for interested individuals to be "aggrieved" parties with the legal right to sue.

"In order to insure that the Federal Power Commission will adequately protect the public interest in the aesthetic, conservational, and recreational aspects of power development, those who by their activities and conduct have exhibited a special interest in such areas must be held to be included in the class of 'aggrieved' parties under s. 313 (b)," Circuit Judge Paul R. Hays wrote in the decision. "We hold that the Federal Power Act gives petitioners a legal right to protect their special interests." He explicitly added that "the preservation of natural beauty and national historic sites" was a basic concern to be considered along with other factors.

It was a revolution in the law. There was absolutely no prior case like it, and it set a precedent that was almost unbelievably broad in its potential applications. Up until then, one could not be deemed an aggrieved party—and therefore could not bring a lawsuit—unless they sustained actual and measurable economic damage. This was the power of David Sive, a brilliant lawyer able to combine classic literature, quoted from memory, with heartfelt passion and emotion, to create powerful—and convincing—legal arguments.

It wasn't always easy to work with Sive, but my time at the firm expanded both the scope of my world as well as what I was capable of professionally. He assumed others could do everything he could, which was a major stretch. In some ways, this was a shortcoming of his. He didn't plan ahead that well, at least when it came to me, which meant I often had to scramble.

"Go to court today," he would tell me in the morning. "We have a motion before the court."

Literally on the spot he would hand me a file, and it would be totally new to me. He expected me to digest the information it contained and be conversant in the case as quickly as he himself would be. It was beyond nerve-wracking. Once he sent me to argue an appeal before the Appellate Division of the Supreme Court of New York, in Brooklyn, and I'd had no time to prepare. It was so embarrassing; I was mortified. He had no understanding of what I was going through, since he could always improvise, no problem.

"Dave, you know I don't know anything about this case," I pleaded with him.

"Oh, it's easy," he said and proceeded to rattle off whatever came into his head as if it were child's play. It would nearly give me a heart attack. But I also knew I was very lucky to be there, learning from a true master.

Moreover, all three partners were good people—generous, smart, and classy. While Sive's background was modest, Neuburger had made a fortune early in his legal career. The parties he threw in his penthouse on Third Avenue and 72nd Street both intimidated and awed me and Susan. We'd never seen so much art, so much wealth, in one person's home. **But none of the partners were out just for money. They truly cared about their clients, and their associates. The partners never nickel and dimed us, and we never had to ask for a raise. It was a given that they would take care of the associates first, before sharing any profit amongst themselves.**

I know now how unusual this kind of caring leadership was. Their generosity set the tone for the firm, and for the way I would manage my own businesses decades later. It also allowed me to upgrade my life with Susan and our growing family. On my new salary, we moved to an apartment of our own in Pelham Manor, just north of the Bronx.

A new era of my life was unfolding, anchored in advocacy and hard work.

CHAPTER 4

The Fight for What's Right: All the Way to the Supreme Court

One of the most influential lessons David Sive taught me was to never give up, no matter what. The work we did at Winer, Neuburger & Sive was about caring for more than just yourself and your own narrow self-interests. It was work that required tremendous compassion and confidence in the righteousness of our cause. This was a firm where most of our energy went into pro bono cases, which were just about all David Sive worked on. He wasn't concerned about money; there were other partners there to give us billable hours on other cases, which paid for the pro bono work. We all made as much money as made us happy, and we had the satisfaction of knowing the firm was making a difference working on some pretty cool things.

Another of the first cases I worked on for Sive was Citizens Committee for the Hudson Valley vs. Volpe. This was an effort to block a proposal to build a six-lane highway on—and in—the Hudson River from the Bronx all the way up to Beacon, New York. The Department of Transportation wanted to fill in a swath of river a couple hundred feet wide to create a bed for a Hudson River Expressway. We represented the Sierra Club, the Village of

Tarrytown, and the Citizens Committee in the suit, and won that one, too. A three-judge panel ruled in 1970 to void an Army Corps permit for landfill and determined that both the dike and causeway would require Congressional approval in order to move forward. Which never happened.

Our cases spanned from local and national to international, especially Committee for Nuclear Responsibility v. Seaborg in 1971. The Atomic Energy Commission (AEC) had decided on Amchitka, an island off Alaska, for a series of nuclear tests, despite the island being part of the Aleutian Islands Wildlife Refuge. Just to give you an idea of how different an era that was, as *The New York Times* reported in 1965, conservationists had recently succeeded in having an Alaska atomic test called off.

"It had been proposed by the Atomic Energy Commission to determine whether nuclear energy was practical for digging harbors," the *Times* drily reported. Nuclear bombs? To dig a big hole? Heck of an idea! What next? Using nukes to build a second Panama Canal?

We sued to enjoin the Amchitka detonation, officially dubbed Project Long Shot. The argument was simple enough: A nuclear blast, even one at the bottom of a mile-deep mine shaft, would spread radioactive material into the environment and be devastating for fish, sea otters, bald eagles, and other wildlife in the region. But the Department of Defense insisted that fallout from the underground test of the Spartan anti-ballistic missile warhead would be minimal.

I remember being in court in Washington with Sive, who was arguing an appeal, and the judge simply detested him. I don't know the judge's politics, especially not compared to today, but at the time he seemed to us like a right-winger; he hated Sive for his outspoken environmental advocacy. He truly believed that Sive was trying to undermine the country's national security by working to prevent nuclear weapons tests. It was very testy in that courtroom.

Sive would keep pushing an argument, and the judge would try to silence him.

"Enough, Mr. Sive," he would declare from the bench.

Sive was always understated, but he was a bulldog, and he kept pushing every limit possible—in his very understated way.

"Yes, Your Honor, I understand," Sive would say, "but I must get this in the record."

Finally, the judge held him in contempt of court.

It was front-page news in *The New York Times* on October 29, 1971: "COURT OF APPEALS REFUSES TO HALT AMCHITKA A-BLAST."

The day before, President Richard Nixon hosted Yugoslav leader Tito at the White House—and issued an order calling for the test to take place, despite our legal challenge. Nixon also received a telegram signed by thirty-four U.S. Senators, both Democrats and Republicans, calling on him not to allow the test. But he held his ground, despite the opposition of both Canada and Japan, arguing that the test was necessary for the U.S. to develop an antimissile system.

"The folly of Amchitka is the folly of a species that burns and poisons and blows up its only home," the *Times* wrote that week in an unsigned editorial.

The blast was scheduled for Saturday, November 6, 1971. The Supreme Court agreed to hold a hearing that morning to consider enjoining the detonation. It was only the second time in the long and august history of that body that they agreed to hold a hearing on a Saturday morning. Sive and I took the train from New York down to Washington. My role was basically to carry his bags and line up papers on the desk in front of us.

I was in total awe, appearing before the Supreme Court on a matter of such importance to the world. Sive had his arguments prepared in his head; he had such incredible recall of everything, but it was my job to sit next to him and line up the case law as Sive responded to questions from the Supreme Court Justices. At that point, they still had quill pens and inkwells for the attorneys, a throwback from a century before. The Justices sat up on a dais, and it was awe-inspiring to see such an iconic lineup: Justices Thurgood Marshall, William O. Douglas, and William J. Brennan—the three who would dissent—and Chief Justice Warren E. Burger, and Justices Harry A. Blackman, Potter Stewart, and Byron R. White. A part of me wanted to cry out, "Holy cow!"

Sive brilliantly presented his case, arguing that upholding "the system of law may be more important than the need for nuclear deterrence." The Solicitor General, Erwin N. Griswold, also deftly made his case, which revolved around the contention that the "balance of deterrence" against the nuclear war with the Soviet Union would be upset if the test did not move forward. As the *Los Angeles Times* reported, "Over repeated objections by Justice Stewart, whom court observers had considered a crucial swing vote, Sive contended the AEC had violated the National Environmental Policy Act by not including warnings about hazards to the environment in its assessment of the test. 'Let's not engage in this rhetoric,' Stewart said. The AEC 'concedes it has the duty to obey the law,' he said."

"There is no situation here of martial law, war emergency, or invasion," Sive told the Court. "We're not dealing with just the matter of another airport, dam, or bridge, but the perils of a five-megaton bomb."

The clock was, nevertheless, ticking. After hearing an hour and a half of arguments, the Court handed down its 4-3 decision shortly before the 12:30 p.m. deadline—scheduled so that the test could proceed four and half hours later. A picture of Sive on the front steps of the Supreme Court made the front page of the next morning's *New York Times*, which of course led with news of the hydrogen bomb blast. I was actually in that photo standing next to David Sive—I still have a copy—but the *Times* cropped me out!

It was front-page news all over the world, a viral news story decades before such a thing existed, though the *San Francisco Examiner*, for example, went with a puckish banner headline: "THE BLAST GOES OFF...THE WORLD GOES ON," next to a large picture from a protest in San Francisco, including one marcher in psychedelic bell bottoms and another carrying a sign reading: "Stop the Bombs / S.E. Asia Amchitka."

It was the biggest U.S. nuclear test in history—and the most bitterly opposed. The five-megaton blast—250 times as powerful as the Hiroshima atomic-bomb explosion—shook the ground with a force equivalent to an earthquake registering 7.0 on the Richter Scale. It triggered twenty-two subsequent earthquakes.

"We feel like hurling plates against the wall," the *New Yorker* magazine wrote that week in a Comment piece:

> Can't anybody ever get the main thing right? And by the main thing we suppose we mean the responsibility—or anyway, the relationship—that should exist by now between leaders and the people they have been asked to lead: the rest of us. … If anyone questions leadership—can't you see?—the whole damn thing will fall apart. Ten thousand or ten million years of human achievement will tumble into nothing. …
>
> Consider the argument of Solicitor General Erwin N. Griswold in favor of the Amchitka test: he said the Supreme Court should not 'second-guess' a decision made by the executive branch, adding that 'grave damage' would be done to the

> security of this country if that should occur. ... On Saturday, when the bomb went off, we thought: You leaders in brown suits and gold braid (sabers dangling against the brown suits), you leaders, with your brave, lonely resolves, your grace under pressure, your glimpses of history—*Stop*. You are monkeying around. It is our place here, and you are just passing through.

The government bragged that the blast went off without a hitch, no radiation leaked, and nothing happened. We now know that, in fact, a lot happened. Scientists estimated that more than 1,000 sea otters died as a result of the detonation. Greenpeace got its start protesting about the Amchitka test and later published information showing that radiation was leaking from the site. In 2002, the U.S. government started mailing out checks for $150,000 to hundreds of Energy Department workers who were exposed to dangerous radiation during that—and two earlier, smaller—nuclear tests on Amchitka.

"'Downwinders,' as mammal biologist Carl M. Hild called people who stayed on Amchitka for extended periods of time, seem to have suffered unusually high levels of diseases linked to radiation exposure," Dean W. Kohlhoff wrote in his 2002 book *Amchitka and the Bomb: Nuclear Testing in Alaska*. "Nick Aleck, who was likely subjected to tritiated water plus an assortment of other radioactive isotopes while working at the test site, later died from radiation-related cancer." And now, fifty years later, the nuclear arms buildup has not abated. The world is overrun with atomic bombs and missiles.

I think back to that day we were before the Supreme Court and how important what we were doing there was. We did not carry the day—we needed one more Justice to do the right thing to stop that hydrogen bomb blast—but in pressing our case, we may have lost the battle and won the war when it came to shifting how people think.

I remember Sive's reaction when we heard the decision had gone against us. He was very understated. He was a man who often showed emotion in his personal life—he cried easily, for example—but not over losses in court. Frankly, he was used to losing. That was just part of it. It was like being an actor or a writer—or an entrepreneur, as I later learned. You just knew most of the stuff you tried would fail. It was the same way in those early days of the environmental movement. **Most of the time we lost, and it was pure doggedness that kept us going. That refusal to give up was in Sive's DNA, and is one of the things he passed on to me. I shared that trait naturally, but he reinforced for me that to accomplish something, you have to work harder than anyone else and never, ever give up.**

Sive's personal qualities also had a profound influence on me. He was kind, generous, and thoughtful. But he did have an ego. I remember when I told him that we'd named our son David, he beamed with pride and thanked us for extending him the honor of naming our first-born son for him. I chuckled: We had three other Davids working at Winer, Neuburger & Sive alone! But he also showed me that you could be very successful and very good at what you did without being selfish or a diva. You don't have to be flamboyant and you don't have to be F. Lee Bailey to succeed. You could be nice.

As things worked out, Sive's legacy is considerably more impressive than F. Lee Bailey's. I think about this sometimes: What are the qualities in a person that add up to a lasting impact? Bailey had a style that would translate well to the present-day thirst for sensation; even after his fall from grace, he might well have shown up as defense counsel in some insanely high-profile case splashed all over social media. But in retrospect, so much of his legal career seems like so much sound and fury, signifying nothing.

Sive was not flashy. But he was determined, he cared, and he was right—about a lot. He fought for his vision, and made a difference that reverberates generations later.

CHAPTER 5

The Start of Entrepreneurship: American Home Shield

I always had a knack for business, but it was my cousin David who turned me into an entrepreneur. He saw potential in me and worked away on me for years. I thought I had done pretty well winding up as a partner at a top Manhattan law firm, working alongside a brilliant idealist like David Sive to try to make a difference in the world—and I had. By 1968, I had saved enough money to buy our first home for $31,000, just up the Hudson River in New City, where our son David was born. Over the next ten years, Susan and I had our third child, Gabby, and in 1978, we sold the house in New City for $65,000 and took out a mortgage to buy a home on two acres in bucolic Chappaqua, Westchester County.

We spent three years looking before we found the property on Roaring Brook Road. For $135,000, we were the new owners of a Colonial-era home that had been renovated once in 1890 and again in the 1950s. There was a barn, a swimming pool, and even a bomb shelter built into a huge rock outcropping behind the house. It needed a lot of work, and the kids were sure it was haunted, but we loved it—it was ours, however briefly.

By that time, Winer, Neuburger & Sive had grown to seven partners, five non-partner lawyer associates, and fifteen or so secretaries and staff. My sixteen years of practicing law had paid off in all ways. But there was another side of the practice, the commercial side, which generated fees to pay our way. That part of the law business was not as much fun.

Hourly billing had become the way we charged for our services, and although I worked ten or twelve hours a day, five days a week—and was racking up as many or more hours than anyone else—I didn't like it. Not that I minded working hard. I didn't. But everyone's measure of value became how many hours they billed a year. I found that objectionable. To me, it wasn't a very nice way to live—and it was at odds with the interests of our clients. The more you billed, the more worth you had to your law partners, but the worse it was for your clients.

One day, as I sat in a meeting with one of our corporate clients, I realized I was thinking about the situation as much from the executives' point of view as I was from the legal standpoint. I was starting to find the challenges of entrepreneurship as intriguing as I'd once found the law. It was time for a change, and I knew just the person to talk to.

My cousin David had been working as a sales manager for Grolier encyclopedia company when he had the idea to start his own company, developing a "Teaching Machine." This was long before personal computers came on the scene. The device was manually operated—a set of paper scrolls printed with prepared lessons that would guide the reader through different areas of study. David threw himself into the work and spent a year knocking on doors to try to line up Wall Street funding.

Eventually, I introduced him to Bob Barsily, a partner at Edward A. Viner and Company, and Bob decided to invest. The

$150,000 he gave David in startup money enabled him to found Scholastic Systems, Inc., which got its start selling the "Teaching Machine." David brought in a group of others from the encyclopedia company, working eighteen hours a day, seven days a week, selling and packing up orders.

"They were looked upon as nuts by their fellow Grolier salesmen and the word passed along in the trade was 'they'll be falling on their face in a couple of months,'" an August 1970 *White Plains Journal News* article explained. "It didn't happen."

Instead, the company prospered and grew to more than 250 employees, all shareholders, which helped ensure that each person felt valued and empowered. I was secretary and counsel, a shareholder, and always an advisor to David. I was his attorney and confidant. He was always pushing the limit, and I always had to tell him, "David, you can't do that," "Do it this way," or "Do it that way." And he relied on that—for a while.

A few years into it, we negotiated a sale of Scholastic Systems to Xerox, and the deal almost went through. It would have been a great payday for all of us. But on the day before we were about to fly up to Rochester, New York to close the sale, some negative publicity about Xerox hit the press and the deal was off. To say that was a disappointment would be an understatement.

But we didn't give up. A short time later, David found another buyer, Cenco Instruments Corporation in Chicago; he sold the company, and netted about half a million dollars. Not bad for a guy in his early thirties at the time. Since I was a shareholder, I did all right in the deal as well.

Though I was still at Winer, Neuburger & Sive, David and I started brainstorming ideas for other companies after that. He had cash on hand, a good Chief Financial Officer, and some good salespeople. He was ready to try again with another company.

I had heard an ad on the radio about a program in New York where if you paid around a hundred dollars a year, you could get guaranteed tradesmen at a big discount, twenty-four hours a day, seven days a week. It sounded great—fix whatever needed repair: plumbing, heating, air-conditioning, electrical systems, kitchen appliances, and washers and dryers. I looked it up and found the company was really a bunch of off-duty firemen and police officers on Long Island who had this going as a side business.

One day David and I were sitting and talking at my house, and I told him about it.

"I think there's something there," I said. "You just made half a million dollars. Let's try to do this ourselves."

So we started working on the idea. I recognized the genius of what the Long Island firemen and police officers were doing and thought we could try it on a bigger scale. Instead of offering a discount on the services, why not charge $200 or $300 a year instead of $100 and provide the services for a nominal, say $25, fee to all subscribers? David was intrigued.

We sent David Palmer, the Scholastic Systems CFO, down to Washington to do research at the Department of Labor Statistics on what it would really cost us to provide all this servicing. He was a very brainy guy and came up with a detailed analysis, which we plotted out on a matrix detailing our probable costs.

That was when we discovered the yearly subscription model would work, and we launched a company called American Home Shield. David was the president, and I was the secretary and outside counsel; the board consisted of David, me, and one other guy. I give David credit: he showed his persistence and ability to connect the dots, which is crucial for creating a business. Until you see those dots connect, you don't know if they ever will.

David could always sell, but he did have a tendency to exaggerate. He was never shy about embellishing a story if he thought it would sound better than the truth. A company history of American Home Shield's first fifty years, 1971-2021, noted that "American Home Shield founded the home warranty industry in 1971," offering the historical backdrop that 1971 was the year that "Walt Disney World opened in Florida, the Apollo 14 mission landed on the moon, Starbucks opened its first coffee shop in Seattle, and American Home Shield was founded." The history went on to credit me—"Sigmund 'Sig' Anderman"—with coming up with the idea for the company after hearing about the Long Island policemen and firemen offering their services.

But since David's motto was "never let the facts get in the way of a good story," early coverage of our new company took a different tack. Based on what David told the *The New York Times* in 1972, here was how the story of American Home Shield's genesis was translated into a *Times* article: "One wintry Sunday a few years ago, David T. Smith—then an executive of an educational materials company—experienced homeowner's trauma. His heating system whimpered to a halt and died. Ten phone calls later, he had reached nine plumbers' answering services and one plumber, who said he thought he might be able to come by Tuesday. In talking about his chilling experience to friends and neighbors, he discovered that his problems were a common malady among homeowners. It was then, he said, that 'the light bulb lit up in my head.'"

Actually, that does sound better than being inspired by a radio program!

The *Times* summed up American Home Shield as, "a repair company that operates much like a medical insurance plan." Subscribers paid a small annual fee—which at the beginning was two or three hundred dollars—and were covered for a variety of homeowner needs: including air-conditioning, electrical, heating and plumbing systems, even roof upkeep. The vast majority of homes would be in good enough shape to be eligible for the service, but some needed repairs or upgrades before they would be accepted. Subscribers could call for help any day of the week, including holidays, and a repair van would be dispatched to the house; two yearly visits for preventative maintenance were also included.

That article came out at a time when our focus was on selling the idea directly to consumers through ads, in newspapers, on flyers, and on the radio, any option we could find. We started with a focus on New Jersey and planned to gradually expand from there, adding areas of subscribers on Long Island, for example.

Startups are never easy. People have no idea what you're offering unless you tell them, and even then, obstacles remain. "It was very, very difficult with American Home Shield," David says now. "Nobody knew. Was American Home Shield a book or a battleship? What's an American Home Shield?"

David went door to door promoting the idea and put the sales team to work. For a lot of people, hearing the pitch sounded good—great even—but there were trust issues. *Would the company survive after I paid them the premium up front? Would it still exist in another year? Or two? Would it deliver the services it promised?*

We would—that part we had covered, but the issue we had with our early business model was that it cost too much to sell the product. We would send an underwriter out to the house of each prospective client and get a full workup on likely costs, offering each client an appropriately adjusted rate. As a result of having to pay the salespeople and the underwriters, we lost money on every sale. It wasn't sustainable. We were about to run out of money. Then came a stroke of plain old good luck.

David ran into a fellow named Ken Berg, head of Berg Agency, a large New Jersey residential real estate company who had just bought two real-estate agencies in Northern California. Ken was one of the more innovative real-estate executives around. Between David and Ken, they came up with the idea of tweaking the product description and offering it as a "one-year home warranty" for resale homes.

Berg suggested we test the idea with one of his two new companies in California—Valley Realty in Dublin, about thirty-five miles east of San Francisco in the East Bay. "If Frank Straface, the president of Valley, likes it, we'll test it there," he said.

David flew out to California to make his pitch. Frank loved the idea, and, as they say, the rest is history. Valley started advertising that, "Every home sold by Valley Realty comes with a one-year warranty." His sales boomed. And so did American Home Shield's.

The *Oakland Tribune* published a September 9, 1973 article on the new collaboration with a large photograph of David and Frank standing behind a Valley Realty sign reading "SOLD" and next to one of our white American Home Shield vans. Painted on the van was a huge version of our logo and the words "ELECTRICAL AIR-CONDITIONING PLUMBING HEATING."

Noting the glaring lack of consumer protection in housing nationally, the article reported: "A progressive Eastbay real estate firm, Dublin-based Valley Reality, is moving ahead on its own, however, in announcing the first warranty program for previously owned homes in the Bay Area. ... Straface emphasized how often the buyer or seller of residential property is faced with unexpected and expensive repairs, and oftentimes long delays to get a repairman out to fix the problem."

Frank told the paper: "Since we've come to expect a warranty on a $3,000 car, certainly the consumer deserves a guarantee with the purchase of his home."

A car for $3,000? That's how it was fifty years ago.

Valley had the home seller pay for the warranty, promising that the home would sell faster and at a higher price—and it did. The strategy was brilliant. Since the warranty was included on every home sale, we avoided the risk that only sellers of "fixer-uppers" would buy the warranty. We also eliminated sales costs—it was illegal to pay commissions to realtors for the sale.

With business booming, soon I was flying out to California at least once a month. My work as counsel for the company grew heavier and heavier. We were expanding all over the country and running into issues with insurance regulators, and every one of the fifty states had its own insurance department. As the warranty became more prominent and visible across the country, insurance commissioners were saying, "Hey, you guys are collecting $300 up front and promising to do work over the next year if something breaks down. You're insurance! You need to keep the $300 in reserve, like an insurance company." I would go around the country talking to insurance commissioners and convincing them, 100 percent of them, that we were not insurance. It was just a service contract, like a refrigerator service contract. That's not insurance.

"Look, it may walk like a duck, and quack like a duck, and swim like a duck," I would argue, "but it's not a duck. It's not insurance."

The company was doing great, but by late 1978—shortly after Susan and I had moved the three kids to our new home in Chappaqua—David was bored with it all. He was into other things. So he made me an offer.

"Sig, you're a smart guy," he said. "You're a good businessman. You're giving me great, sound advice. Why don't you come to California and join the company? You can be president, and I'll be CEO?"

I turned down David's first offer. It was a fun idea, giving up everything to move out to California. Those were years when pop music was actively celebrating a new way of life out on the Coast. You know, "If you're going to San Francisco, be sure to wear some flowers in your hair," and that kind of thing.

But I was reluctant to leave behind the stability of life as a partner at a great New York law firm. The money was good, and Susan and I had a very comfortable life. How could I give all that up?

Eventually, it was California itself that decided the issue. I needed to fly out regularly for board and business meetings, so I took Susan with me on some visits to San Francisco and we had a spectacular time together. We strolled and shopped in the storybook village of Carmel and walked on the white-sand beach past glorious Monterey Cypress trees. We rented a sailboat and sailed on San Francisco Bay. We went skiing up at Squaw Valley in Lake Tahoe. All in one week!

If it sounds magical, it was. Northern California was very seductive to both of us. Of course, when you're visiting a place, taking it in for the first time, that's a lot different than when you're living there and working there and driving your kids to school and dentist appointments and taking care of them when they're sick. For us, exploring California felt like a wonderful vacation. There was a huge allure to the place—and to the idea of taking on exciting new challenges.

I mulled it over for at least six months and eventually came around. I decided I was ready to take the leap, but wasn't sure what to say to Susan to bring her around. I needn't have worried. She was a step ahead of me.

"They asked me again to come out and run the company," I told her. "Susan, I think I could do this job."

"Why don't we give it a try?" she said.

So we did.

We moved to California in summer 1979, and I took over as president of American Home Shield. My timing was not great. The energy crisis of 1979 led to the financial crisis of 1980, with the country entering a recession in January 1980. The real-estate market tanked. The number of home sales, on which our revenues depended, tanked. Our revenues dropped dramatically and insurance regulators were all over us. It was harrowing.

Ours was a cash-flow business. If your client base was expanding, your cash flow was good and you had ample liquid funds from yearly subscriptions to handle the costs of servicing past contracts. If, on the other hand, bleak economic times led to a drop in your subscription base, then the opposite was true and you would have to struggle just to cover past contracts. That was where we found ourselves. We weren't required to maintain cash reserves and didn't have any!

I was scrambling to find new investors for the company. I spent almost a year trying to convince people to invest in us. I flew to New York, to Chicago, to London. No takers. And we were quickly running out of money. It was one of the most stressful times of my life. We were struggling to meet payroll every two weeks, and I didn't think we would make it.

Once again, we got lucky. But I knew, as the Roman philosopher Seneca once said, "Luck is what happens when preparation meets opportunity." We were prepared, and opportunity knocked: In 1981, we sold American Home Shield to a small group of individual investors for about $20 million. And a few years after that, it sold to Service Master L.P. for $80 million.

The company is still successful, more than fifty years after David and I came up with the idea, and it is listed on NASDAQ with a valuation of about $3 billion. But we had quite a ways to go to get there.

Life as an
Entrepreneur
and the
Billion-Dollar
Idea

CHAPTER 6

No Going Back: Creating CompuFund

It was American Home Shield that brought me to California, but even after we sold the company, I knew there was no going back. I wasn't going back to New York—and I wasn't going back to law. A California sense of wide-open possibility had kicked in, and I was going to see where it would take me. If I had been back in New York, I might not have been so focused on looking at how new technologies could solve old problems, but in Northern California, that mindset was in the air all around me.

I wanted to take advantage of that sense of possibility, and I knew I needed to step up my own leadership skills along the way—particularly as I transitioned from a career in law to a professional life in business. I sought the advice of a former law school classmate who'd made a similar career move. He suggested I read a few books about management and entrepreneurship that had helped him, particularly the work of Peter Drucker—who many consider the founder of modern management. Drucker's books—and the example of others I'd worked for, like my own father, David Sive, and Ralph Neuburger—helped me define not just the kind of business I wanted to run, but the kind of leader I wanted to be. I was ready for a new chapter.

Looking back from the 21st century, it's hard to convey what it was like in the days before personal computers, smartphones, email, and the Internet opened up so many new ways of living and doing business. The term "cyberspace" was not even invented until 1984 when it was coined by *Neuromancer* author William Gibson. That was one year after the creation, by the Domain Name System, of .com, .org, .net, .edu and other TLDs, or top-level domain names. A race was on to see who could come up with the best ideas for how to make life easier for people—and this was great for business.

Susan and I had now been through the elaborate home-buying process twice in New York, and we were about to go through it all over again out West. Like everyone trying to buy a house in those years, we were constantly struck by how complicated, confusing and aggravating it all was. Especially getting a mortgage. Interest rates were much higher and much more variable back then, with criteria so convoluted no layperson could begin to understand it all. **I was curious how these new technological tools we were just learning about could help the individual consumer grapple with comparison shopping for a good deal on a mortgage and help reduce stress levels all around.**

"What was incredible to me when I started looking into it," I recalled to the *Los Angeles Times* in June 1984, "was that there was no real estate lender that I could find who had come up with a loan-processing system that took advantage of modern electronics. They were still writing everything out by hand and wearing green eyeshades."

I never thought of myself as a visionary or even much of an early adopter when it came to computers, but I guess in hindsight, I was. What seemed normal to me at the time was, in fact, well ahead of the curve.

At American Home Shield, given the complexities of our customer call center and service dispatch operation, particularly with David's ad hoc style, we would have been lost if we hadn't brought in a first-rate computer programmer in the late 1970s. Fortunately, we had hired a young ex-cop from Chicago named Bob Giles, who happened to be a whiz with computers. He was then in his thirties, and became our director of Management Information Systems.

Bob set up American Home Shield so that we computerized the process of receiving calls from policyholders and dispatching contractors to drive out and make repairs. He programmed a fantastic system where a customer would call in, and on the screen you could type in the customer's name, phone number, contract number, or address. Up popped all the details of the customer's coverage, which for us tended to run the gamut. David, god bless him, would travel around the country to sign up more realtors, and of course, he would improvise to get deals done. He might be in Topeka meeting with the president of Kansas Real Estate, who oversaw three offices of real-estate agents.

"I'll buy it," the guy might say, then add, "but I'll only buy it if you cover televisions, because last week my television went out, and I couldn't get a television repairman."

"Sure, we'll cover televisions for you," David would tell him— or whatever he had to say that a potential customer needed to hear to close a deal.

Before Bob Giles brought us into the computer age, we had warehouse space in Dublin, California, where the walls were covered with sheets of paper marked up with all the quirky specifics of each contract, whether it was a TV service in Kansas, a price break for Century 21 in Florida, or coverage for indoor whirlpool spas for one of our California clients. The procedure back then was for a customer support person to look up, down, and across the walls of that warehouse space, festooned with a forest of paper, until they found the sheet for a particular policy; they could then find the customer's deductible or basic information like the zip code of whatever service provider was closest to Topeka.

Although younger generations today take lightning speed information for granted, we were amazed back then at the ability of this technology. By 1979, important information was just a keystroke away, and it was magnificent. Once you had an individual client's account up on the screen, you had access to all the information you needed, including background on which contractors had performed well—or poorly—on a previous service, or which realtor was trying to game the system by only offering American Home Shield on high-risk houses and fixer-uppers. Bob's brilliant program also gave us updated information on each realtor, including profit-and-loss statements.

Given the solution we came up with for home warranties, I knew that computers could play a role in helping consumers find and get better loans. When I was still president of American Home Shield, I was buying a new Jeep and was about to sign the paperwork on a car loan at an interest rate of 12.5 percent when a friend tipped me off to a better deal. He steered me to another bank offering 10.5 percent, and I was thrilled. Not only did I get help from a friend, but that experience showed me there was a market for quick, accurate information on available loans.

In 1982, the year after we sold American Home Shield, I was talking to Frank Straface of Valley Realty in the San Francisco Bay area, kicking around ideas on what to do next.

"These adjustable rate mortgages are driving us crazy," he told me.

Just a few months earlier, the Federal Reserve had dropped

interest rates half a percentage point, to 11.5 percent. Because interest rates were so high at the time, the average rate for a thirty-year mortgage in 1982 was over 16 percent. Consumers were having a hard time qualifying for a mortgage at those rates, so banks became creative—they invented adjustable-rate mortgage loans with low starting rates that would adjust upward periodically.

Every bank had its own novel formula, with different start rates, adjustment periods, and indexes upon which the actual interest rate would be based. Savings and Loan Associations, the only institutions allowed to offer mortgages until the mid-1980s, were offering so many variations: one adjustable rate loan would adjust every three months to the LIBOR (London Interbank Offered Rate), another would adjust every month to the T-Bill rate, and yet another would stay the same for two years but start at a higher rate. Borrowers were getting lost in a blizzard of numbers from 6 to 18 percent, depending on the fine print.

A Knight-Ridder article that year, headlined "MAZE AWAITS THE BUYER," explained: "Home financing used to be so simple. Call three lenders, pick the best rate. Not anymore. Today, home buyers face a bewildering choice of financing plans. Adjustable rates, graduated payment rates, wraparounds, rapid payment mortgages, graduated equity loans, blended mortgages, negative amortization. The lenders' shorthand—ARM, GPM, WRAP, RPM, GEM—is enough to give consumers cold feet. It even confuses the experts."

Frank Straface told me his customers at Valley Realty would regularly ask: "Which loan is the best for me?"

And he would have to answer: "I have no idea."

"The consumer now faces an absolute maze of different loan instruments with different rates, different terms, different adjustable criteria, and different indexes to which loans are keyed," I explained to the Sunday *San Francisco Examiner* in 1984. "There literally are hundreds of varieties of mortgages and the home-buyer doesn't know where to start to get information to compare one loan with another for the best deal. There are over 4,000 loan packages being offered in the state. By the time a homebuyer goes through only ten programs, he or she will be totally confused."

I thought back to the amazing difference computers had made for us with American Home Shield and realized it might be worth exploring whether the mortgage-loan mess could also be cleaned up through computer programs. I decided to test the idea out with a group of people I knew would see value in the project, and stand to benefit from it themselves—realtors. Right off the bat, ten or fifteen from big firms said they loved the concept, and urged me to do it.

Putting up some seed money myself, I went back to that same group and asked if they wanted to invest in the startup. Knowing it had the potential to expand their business, they were thrilled to pitch in. I came up with a figure for a company valuation, and offered them a certain number of shares for their contribution. We were up and running.

I founded CompuFund National Mortgage Network, Inc. in 1982, and hired Bob Giles' deputy, Bruce Baker, asking him to get creative and program a comparative rate sheet that would have reliable, up-to-date information. "Here's what I'd like to do," I told Bruce. "I want to get all those rates and programs and basically come up with a simple mortgage comparison sheet that describes multiple loans side-by-side, so borrowers can compare 'apples to apples.'"

It took a while to work out just what that would mean, but Bruce got to work programming, and the first version of Compu-Fund came out great. Realtors couldn't wait to sign up for the CompuFund Mortgage Passport. Back then, most realtors had what were known as "dumb terminals"—computers that were just screens, with no computing power or data, linked over telephone lines to a central mainframe computer at the local Multiple Listing Service (MLS) headquarters. They would log into the MLS system to look up all the homes for sale on the screen. When a realtor got a listing, the information would have to be typed into the MLS screen and then forwarded by connecting to the MLS mainframe by modem, usually via an acoustic coupler into which a telephone handset was cradled.

I got the idea to ask the MLS companies in the San Francisco Bay Area to let us hook into their computer system, keep our data on their mainframes, and let realtors dial in to get our CompuFund rates and Mortgage Passport. Realtors liked that approach, as they would only have to learn one method to access both their real-estate and mortgage data. At first the MLS companies all resisted. But after maybe six months of arguing our case, I finally got the biggest MLS company in the country, Planning Research Corporation, to agree. One of our salespeople, Claudia Thomas, had been working for the MLS company, so we had her selling this to both the MLS companies and realtors.

CompuFund was a game-changer. Our research showed that lenders were changing both the rates and the terms of their programs every eight days, on average. We found that even if an individual borrower called up different branches of the same lender, they would often receive contradictory information. People wanted to be saved from all that. I hired half a dozen clerks to call the banks—Home Savings, American Savings, and Lincoln Savings and Loan—every day to stay on top of any changes in rates or criteria. We brought simplicity, clarity, and accurate information where before there was mostly chaos.

I started out asking realtors for $60 a month to use the service and encountered no resistance. Within six months, I upped that to $70 a month and still, no resistance. Soon we were charging realtors

$90 a month, and the service was selling like hotcakes. In the first year of operations, we signed up over a thousand realtors. At $90 a month each, it became a thriving business. And we were on track to double that in the second year.

It was all going so well, and then one of the realtors we were working with surprised me with a suggestion.

"You're doing so much already," he said. "Why don't you just process the loans as well?"

I had not thought of becoming a mortgage broker. Interesting idea. I looked into it and was surprised to find that up until then, processing the loans was not even automated. A typist would actually roll forms into a typewriter—like the 1003 Universal Residential Loan Application Form—and type out all the information.

"Why don't we just start computerizing this?" I asked Bruce Baker. "We can type in the data and let the computer print out the application. We could cut costs, pass the savings on to the customer, and gain a real competitive advantage."

That's exactly what we did. And it worked.

Our income jumped. We gathered all the documents and data necessary to get a mortgage funded, check the borrower's creditworthiness and background, get the property appraised, put the package together, and submit the entire paper bundle to a lender for funding. When the loan was funded, the lender (a Savings and Loan association usually) would pay us a fee for our services. Because we were also a mortgage broker, instead of getting $90 a month per client, we also cleared $1,000 or more on each loan after paying a loan officer $500 and covering overhead.

Business was so good, in fact, that representatives of the big Savings and Loans that brokered our loans would come to town and wine and dine me to get our business. They made all kinds of promises.

"You're our best customer, so you are going to get the best service," they would say. "Whatever you need, just call."

We were advertising in different newspapers and getting good press. An early ad in the *San Francisco Examiner* read, "BALLOON PAYMENT WORRIES? If you're a homeowner confronted with a balloon payment and need help, call us today. CompuFund Mortgage Services, Inc." In 1984 alone, I showed up talking about our services in newspapers from the *Ashbury Park Press* in New Jersey and *Montgomery Advertiser* in Alabama to the *Newark Advocate* in Ohio, the *Salt Lake Tribune* in Utah, and the *Calgary Herald* in Canada.

It was too good to last, I can say now, looking back. In 1984, something went haywire with American Savings, our primary lender. As interest rates dropped from unparalleled highs, and their volume began to soar, the same people who had told me to call any time, whatever I needed, stopped returning my calls. It was head-spinning.

Time is of the essence in the mortgage game. Realtors are on pins and needles waiting to hear back, and the borrower wants an answer as soon as possible. But suddenly, instead of getting a twenty-four-hour turnaround on approval packages as we previously had from American Savings, forty-eight or seventy-two hours would go by without a peep from them.

Realtors were calling me at home to find out when their client's loan would be approved. And I couldn't answer them. But the lesson I learned from my work with David Sive was that just when it seemed like everything was going wrong, that was the time to persevere. Despite our challenges, I was not going to give up now, and good thing I didn't.

CHAPTER 7

The Power of Connection: Saving CompuFund

I'd had enough. We had an excellent roster of real-estate firms as clients, including McGarvey Clark, Coldwell Banker, Fox & Carskadon, Grubb & Ellis, John M. Grubb, Wells & Bennett, and Sterpa Realty. I needed to look for solutions on the banking side, so I wouldn't have to rely on the likes of American Savings. I was out to lunch with my friend J. Carter Witt, a veteran mortgage banker who was with Mason-McDuffie for thirty years, including twelve years as executive vice president of its Northern California division. In February 1983, Carter joined our board.

"Sig, why don't you just become a lender?" Carter said. "You be the lender."

It didn't sink in at first.

"Be a banker?" I asked.

That seemed like a big step.

"What would actually be involved?" I asked Carter.

"Well, you'll just process the loan like you have been, and then fund the loan yourself instead of brokering out to another lender," he said.

He made it sound so simple.

"You'll get a warehouse line," he said, using the term for a line of credit provided to a loan originator. "You'll be able to borrow. Then you'll fund the loans yourself and you sell them directly to Fannie Mae and Freddie Mac. You don't need American Savings. When you get the proceeds from the loan sale, you pay back the warehouse lender, and keep the profit for yourself."

I thought: Well that sounds like a great idea. It was worth a try. I happened to be friends with a guy named Preston Martin, a former California savings and loan commissioner who basically invented private mortgage insurance. He founded PMI Mortgage Insurance Co. in 1972, and later sold it to Sears for a reported $5 million. President Reagan appointed Martin vice chairman of the Federal Reserve Board in 1982, and he made headlines for openly clashing with Fed Chairman Paul Volcker.

I knew I needed good advice if I wanted to get into lending, so I went over to San Francisco to see Preston in his office in the iconic Transamerica Pyramid, at 601 Montgomery Street. Preston, being a kind person, was happy to offer me advice.

"If you want to be a lender, then you should talk to Jeff Babcock," Preston told me. "Jeff just left PMI as the head of sales, and he's the most knowledgeable person I know in the mortgage industry."

So I went to see Jeff. He was smart as a whip, with a charm that distracted from a prominent stammer. I liked him right off the bat. He seemed to live up to Preston Martin's description. Jeff knew everything and everybody in the mortgage business. He walked me through what I would need, in abundant detail, to become a lender: Capital. We would need a lot of capital. We would need a line of credit. But when it came to collecting loan payments, or servicing, we would farm out the work to someone else, who would actually buy the rights to do the job for us.

"You need somebody to buy the servicing from you because that's how you get cash flow," Jeff explained. "Somebody's going to pay you for the servicing because, crazy as it sounds, it's very profitable. The way mortgages work, Fannie Mae takes their interest rate. Another three-eighths of a percent goes to the servicer. That's about $750 per year on a $200,000 loan. And performing the servicing only costs about $80 a year. So people want to buy those rights."

A typical thirty-year home loan might stay on the books an average of nine years, so the servicer has incentive to pay you thousands of dollars up front to take that on for you. It was paying off to have cultivated strong friendships with people who could steer me in the right direction.

What's more, Jeff had a friend at PMI, Roger Lindland, who had just taken over as CEO of Great American Bank in San Diego.

"Let's pitch him and see what he says," he suggested. "It's a trial run. We'll see what he thinks about your whole idea about computerized mortgages being the future."

We showed up for the meeting in San Diego to make the pitch, and for the first half an hour, Gordon Luce, who was chairman of the board of Great American, kept pointing to a TV monitor he had in his grand office and asking me to take another look. It was a live feed showing peregrine falcons up on the roof of his bank building.

"This is Perry and this is Mimi, and they're mating," he told me.

Look, who wasn't interested in peregrine falcons mating? I'd have gladly talked about them all day long. But this was a pitch meeting, and I wanted to get to the point. As anxious as I was to move forward, the power of kindness was with me. I smiled. I listened. I smiled some more. At least thirty minutes went by as we discussed the mating falcons.

Gordon Luce was a great guy, warm, friendly, and charming,

part of Ronald Reagan's famous "Kitchen Cabinet" when he was the governor of California. Born in San Diego to an old California family—his grandfather, Moses, wrote the charter for San Diego's first Savings and Loan institution—Gordon was close friends with Reagan. As his friend Jim Schmidt, also in the meeting that morning, later put it to the Los Angeles Times, "They had such great chemistry."

Besides Roger, Gordon, and Jim, the president of the mortgage division, it was Jeff and me making the pitch. I was a little keyed up, so when Jeff would try to make a point, I would get impatient and jump in with my own ideas.

The meeting seemed to be going well, but I really wasn't sure. This was all new to me. It sounded like they loved the idea of computerizing the mortgage process and were impressed with the system we had come up with. It was, after all, a revolutionary step forward in the mortgage industry.

"We have to break for lunch," Roger eventually said. "But before you go, tell me how much capital you really think you need."

We said we needed $2.5 million.

"What else do you need to run this?" Gordon asked.

"We need someone to purchase our servicing rights, and a warehouse line of credit," I replied.

"How much of a warehouse line do you need?" Gordon asked.

Gordon had taken over San Diego Federal Savings in 1969 as a tiny thrift and turned it into the eighth-largest savings and loan in the country, an innovator in the field. I could see he was actively interested, not just breezing through formalities. They were ready to get serious with us.

"Jeff, what do you think?" I said, handing it over to the expert.

Jeff started and stopped a couple times. When he got excited, his stammer got worse, and he took longer and longer to get out a sentence. He was losing his audience. Roger and Jim were looking out the window. They looked hungry. Gordon Luce was looking at his falcons. I couldn't let the moment pass.

"All right," I said, taking charge. "You're a bank, you've got nearly unlimited funds, and you see our growth potential. We need an unlimited warehouse line."

Then we all went to lunch. Jeff and I were down on the street, a block away, about to grab a bite at a luncheonette when he turned to me with a pained look on his face.

"You're a f-f-f," he began, and then blurted it out. "F-f-f-fucking i-i-i-diot."

I stared back at him.

"You can't ask a bank for all their money," he scolded me. "You've got to tell them how much."

"What should I have told them?" I asked.

"Twenty-five million, maybe thirty," Jeff said.

"But why didn't you tell me that beforehand?"

"I didn't think they would ask," Jeff said. "This was only supposed to be a practice run, to see how the story sounded. It wasn't a sales call."

Lunch was tense. I headed back to Gordon's office with sweaty palms, eager to reconvene and see what the falcons were up to.

"Sig, we're very impressed with your program," Gordon started.

I was waiting for the "but." It didn't come.

"Don't look any further," Gordon continued. "We think we can handle everything. We would like to invest $2.5 million for 20 percent of the company. We'll buy your servicing from you and pay you 2 percent of the value of the loan up front."

That was huge. I waited for the rest. I didn't want to blink.

"But we can't give you an unlimited warehouse line," he said, and

I was ready for Jeff to start kicking my shin under the table. "By our charter, we could only lend one borrower a hundred million dollars."

A hundred million? A hundred million! We'd done it.

CHAPTER 8

On the Brink of Bankruptcy

I opened up my mail one day not long after that, and found myself staring at a note for a $100 million warehouse line of credit that looked a lot like a check. I held it in my hands and kept staring: $100,000,000.

I remember calling my dad, who had set an example of kindness and determination throughout my life. He and my mother had recently moved from Spring Valley to a senior community in Waldwick in Bergen County, New Jersey. It was 1984, and my father had just turned seventy-four. After working from the time he was ten, he had finally retired a couple years earlier. It was well deserved. After graduating high school, he went to work in a cleaning store in Greenwich Village, then opened his own shop a few years later. By 1953, the negative effects of daily contact with dry cleaning fluid fumes became pronounced. He sold the store and moved the family to Spring Valley.

My parents tried their hand in the retail business in Spring Valley with Anderman Apparel, but it flopped after a few struggling years. In hindsight, it was doomed to fail, as my parents knew nothing about fashion—or retailing. My dad needed to get a job and applied for a clerk position in the local unemployment office in Spring Valley. Fifteen years later, he retired as manager of the office. Sadly, soon after retiring, he contracted leukemia. After some aggressive chemotherapy, he was in remission—for the second time. He remained upbeat and optimistic, and we spoke every day.

"Dad, you're not going to believe what I have here in front of me," I told him.

It felt so unreal that I thought talking to my father might make it hit home for me.

"I'm holding a promissory note for a hundred million dollars," I told my dad. "I've never seen so many zeroes in my life."

I thought my father would be happy for me. Excited. Instead he was confused. And worried. He had worked seven days a week all through my childhood just to survive. Every penny was precious.

"What does that mean?" he asked. "You owe them the money?"

He was missing the point.

"Yes, Dad, but it's owed by the corporation, not me personally," I tried to explain.

"Siggy, don't sign it," he said. "Don't get yourself in debt."

"Dad," I said, about to try to persuade him again, then thought twice. Given how difficult it had been for him to earn money over so many decades, I understood how he would view that hundred million dollar promissory note differently than me.

I signed. I knew this was the right path.

I thought of that moment again later that year, in September, when my father died. The leukemia came back, and this time there was no remission. Just a steady decline. My mother, my sisters and I, my aunt Sarah (my dad's older sister), and all nine of his grandchildren gathered as a family for the burial at Beth El Cemetery in Washington Township, New Jersey.

I thought of his mother's courage in making the move from

Buchach to America with only five bucks and a lot of hope, and the possibilities that it created for us. I thought about how hard my dad worked—from the time he graduated from high school—to eke out a living and provide us with a better life than he had ever experienced. He did so without a complaint, without anger or resentment. He was the kindest, most hardworking man you'd ever meet.

My father's death was an enormous rite of passage. In the years that followed, more loss would visit me—reminding me of the many responsibilities I held, both within my family and my community. My life, and the business I now ran with hundreds of employees, may have looked a lot different than my father's. But it was his love, concern, and kindness that empowered me to keep pushing ahead—even when I was heading into uncharted territory.

The best part of the deal with Great American Bank was that we were excited to be working with Gordon Luce and his team, and they were excited to be working with us. It felt historic. As Gordon told one Southern California newspaper in a March 1984 article announcing the deal, "We believe the concept of computerized loan selection, origination and processing is on the threshold of a dramatic expansion. It provides an important real-time link between real-estate brokers and lenders."

We'd become a real lender. I couldn't believe what I saw when I drove out to the American Savings loan-processing center in Stockton, California—an hour east of our CompuFund offices in Dublin—to pick up our loan files so we could begin to fund loans ourselves. Some of these files were piled high on desks, sheaves of disordered papers stuffed several inches thick into Manilla folders. Back in those days, there were plenty of cigarette smokers, and you would see folders with holes burned into them by cigarette butts.

Crazy! I thought. *This is how how the biggest bank in the country does this? We're going to computerize everything, eliminate paper, and change the way mortgages are done in America.*

CompuFund started working on automating the process. Over the next year, as we completed automation, we kept growing. And as our loan volume grew, I flew down to San Diego for meetings more and more often, at least twice a month. We were funding 30 to 100 loans a day, at an average of about $100,000 per loan. Great American was providing the warehouse line of credit to allow us to fund the loans and then buying the loans themselves. It added up fast.

Staying on top of all those transactions got very complicated. Every day we were funding loans, selling loans, and getting receipts on loans we had sold twenty-five or thirty days before. We had to clear our warehouse line. We had to sell the loans to another department at Great American. There were a lot of moving parts that needed constant monitoring.

I insisted on a policy of balancing our checkbook every day. Maybe I was my father's son in that regard: I was always afraid some money might suddenly vanish. If you had $100 million dollars floating around, some clerk might get a little tempted and think: *Hmmm, maybe I'll just borrow a thousand dollars for today, and forget to pay it back.* And maybe the thousand would become ten thousand, and then a lot more than that. We balanced our checkbook every day, and had auditors come in every single month to go over everything and make sure it was all kosher. And it all was—until it wasn't.

"There's $3 million missing," one of our controllers told me one day. "Great American says they sent us the money. We never got it."

I was on a plane to San Diego that day. I met with Jim Schmidt at Great American and told him about the $3 million discrepancy. It was news to him. Great American had not noticed anything amiss.

"Well, let's check it out," I said.

It took them a month before they came back to me with an explanation.

"We made that deposit to the wrong account," Jim explained.

What? The wrong account? That sounded like an easy problem to fix.

"What kind of account?" I asked.

He seemed reluctant to tell me.

"Well, it was a small depositor," Jim finally explained. "An old couple in San Diego."

I was not catching on to the problem.

"Well, just get it back from them," I suggested.

"We can't," Jim said.

"Why not?"

Jim was all but squirming with awkwardness.

"First of all, they said that they never had more than $300 in their bank account," he told me. "They were always living hand to mouth. They belonged to the Crystal Cathedral, they were very religious, and they prayed every day that one day they would get rich. So when they saw the $3 million arrive in their account, they just assumed it was an answer to their prayers. Clearly God had intervened. So they bought a car and a house and a lot of stuff for about a million dollars, but then they gave $2 million to the Crystal Cathedral."

The Reformed Church of America's Crystal Cathedral in Orange, California, which opened in 1980, was billed as "the largest glass building in the world." The church was founded in 1955 by Christian televangelist Robert Schuller, who would go on to host the *Hour of Power* TV show for forty years.

"So just get the money back," I suggested to Jim. "It's ill-gotten gains. Should be straightforward."

"We can't," he said. "We're an Orange County and San Diego bank. If news ever got out that we tried to take $2 million from the

Crystal Cathedral, our business would be blasted."

What could we do? Perhaps that money was going to a good cause. Maybe it was helping people in need. I was in the business of kindness—not that I didn't need the money for the business, but I supposed that if it was going to go anywhere, accidentally going to two impoverished people who donated most of it to the church wasn't the worst thing that could have happened. I later learned that Great American recovered their losses from their insurance company. Another example of the power of kindness (and karma). Welcome to the banking business!

It was a wonderful time of feeling the wind at our backs. We'd ventured boldly into new territory in the industry, and we were being rewarded for it. We finished 1984 with 25 percent more growth than we'd planned for that year, with a continuing surge forecast for the following year. Our loan volume rose from $10 million per month in 1983 to more than $50 million per month in 1984. We were quickly approaching the volume of Countrywide Home Loans, which was founded fifteen or twenty years previously and was the number one non-bank mortgage lender in the country.

"Our computerized loan selection and processing business system is now recognized by both home buyers and realtors and mortgage brokers for its win/win advantages," I told the *San Francisco Examiner* in January 1985. "Consumers have the advantages of much wider loan selection with the benefits of competitive loan offerings and faster, more efficient processing service."

By February 1986, *The New York Times* explained, "Shopping by computer is becoming increasingly common in the home mortgage market. Real estate brokers sometimes describe computerized loan origination networks as 'financial blind-dating services,' linking the customer with a national network of lenders. In some cases, these services provide buyers with more favorable mortgage terms than are available in the local market, and the computer may also shorten the closing process by a couple of weeks."

The *Times* focused on Shelternet, a Long Island–based company, and CompuFund, identifying us as "No. 1 and 2 in the field," which was brand new and quickly evolving. The *Times* cited estimates that "computer-generated loans" accounted for roughly 1 percent of the market in 1985 but would grow to 25 percent by 1990.

"The credit verification process, often a notorious sand trap, is accelerated by automation," the *Times* observed.

As it turned out, Shelternet was formed by the Multiple Listing Service who first agreed to share their data center with us. It was a big company, and they apparently liked our idea so much, they copied it—and became a competitor! It really didn't hurt our business, and actually added to the buzz in the real estate industry that computerizing the mortgage process was the way to go.

CompuFund kept growing. Eventually Roger and Jim came to me with the idea of CompuFund taking over the entire mortgage operation of Great American Bank and all its branches around the country. It made good business sense all around. Our system could process loans more efficiently and at a lower cost than their mortgage department could. Realtors were happier working with us, so we had slowly but surely, region by region, assumed the responsibility to process more and more of their loans. Great American owned 30 percent of CompuFund at that point, with Union Bank of Los Angeles owning another 30 percent. Now Great American decided to buy the rest.

It was a terrific deal for me and the other shareholders of CompuFund. All my hard work was paying off, with Great American offering to buy us for cash or their stock—our choice. All the other shareholders of CompuFund took cash. I decided to take stock in this stable New York Stock Exchange-listed bank, so that I could sell my shares periodically over time and avoid hefty capital gains taxes.

To set the scene, as the *Los Angeles Times* later wrote, "In the mid-1980s, Great American Bank seemed to have it all. Chairman Gordon Luce, a politically well connected and socially prominent Republican, had built the San Diego-based savings and loan into one of the industry's powerhouses. By the end of 1985, Luce had grown it to 117 branches and $8.2 billion in assets, up from three offices and $300 million in assets when he joined the thrift, then known as San Diego Federal, in 1969."

I was sitting pretty. The company I founded just four years earlier had been bought by one of the most prestigious banks in the country, run by one of the most impressive and honest executives in the field. Then in 1986, the *Los Angeles Times* described:

> Luce and Great American took a wrong turn, perhaps a fatal one, by acquiring Home Federal Savings of Tucson. What was designed as a bid to dramatically expand the scope of Great American's branches and business activities instead has brought the S&L [Savings & Loan], with its 213 branches and $15.9 billion in assets, to the brink of insolvency. ... Hindsight enables anyone to observe that Great American's move across state lines into Arizona had all the makings of a debacle because it overlooked the principle that successful real-estate lending is built on management's firsthand knowledge of local markets.

The Arizona acquisition turned out to be a fatal move for Great American, true, but it was only part of the picture. This was an honest company with great management. Gordon Luce was a pillar of the community. There were never any accusations of monkeying around with the books or anything like that. They didn't even want to risk hurting anyone's feelings by asking for that $2 million back from the Crystal Cathedral.

We had a top New York law firm advising us, and when I asked them to look into Great American before they bought out Compu-Fund, they told me this was one of the best companies you could ever sell to. "You don't have to do much due diligence," they said. "We have all their SEC records. They're clean as a whistle."

Great American's demise was triggered when the federal government suddenly changed the accounting rules governing S&Ls. In 1989, Congress passed legislation designed to shore up the troubled S&L sector, where many institutions had failed because of reckless practices. That was not Great American. But they got caught up in the cross-currents. As financial columnist Claire Schechter put it in a June 1989 column, "In a major shift from current S&L accounting practices, 'goodwill' (intangible assets without market value) will not be counted toward federal requirements."

Goodwill had been around for years as an accounting concept in the banking industry. It was the accepted order. So, for example, if you bought a bank for $20 million, and it had $15 million in hard assets and no liabilities, the $5 million you paid over and above the hard assets—based on your knowledge that it was a growing business, and you had the expectation of revenue growth—was classified as goodwill. You bought goodwill. It was treated as an asset.

The accounting rules changed overnight, and banks that one day were fully capitalized the next day did not have enough assets to satisfy the newly defined capital requirements. Big banks all over the state of California and all over the country were being put into receivership—and it was stupid.

"Don't worry," Roger and Jim at Great American told me. "It's only a process. We'll get out of it. We'll figure it out."

But they couldn't figure it out.

"We're not going to get out of this," Gordon finally told me. "These guys are serious. Even Reagan can't help us out of this one. So why don't we sell your business back to you?"

I loved the idea. They offered to maintain our warehouse line for a year and a half while we lined up other funding. Great. I got to work and lined up funding to buy back CompuFund. We worked out the terms of a fair deal. Whatever they paid me, I would pay them back. We signed the deal. Clinked glasses in celebration. And then, within hours, the deal was nixed—the federal government decided to block it for no good reason at all.

And that was the end of CompuFund.

It was devastating. I lost everything. We had about twenty shareholders in CompuFund who had invested early, and they all sold their stock to cash out. I never did. I was the biggest shareholder and now that stock was worthless. Susan and I suddenly couldn't pay the mortgage on our house in the East Bay. I went to the bank and asked for forgiveness, but they weren't as forgiving as they are now.

I was scrambling, maxing out my credit cards, loading up one card to pay the next, getting cash advances. I flew to New York to try to make something happen, and didn't have enough money to book my flight home; my sister had to lend me the money for airfare. Susan and I went to a bankruptcy attorney to ask what we could do to forestall foreclosure on the mortgage.

It was wildly embarrassing. I never felt so helpless in my life, and knew that I had to come up with an idea. **I had no choice—I couldn't give up, but what I remembered from my father, my grandmother,**

and from David Sive was that it wasn't about the "wins," it was about not giving up. It was about persevering, despite adversity. Still, it was so stressful for us both, especially Susan.

I was under so much pressure, I didn't think I would find a way out.

CHAPTER 9

Failure, the Key to Success

I was in limbo for almost a year, and it was horrible. Great American Bank was big enough that it took time to fail, and during the period they were in receivership, I had to wind down CompFund. Looking back on scenes from those months feels like recalling a bad dream—especially the day we auctioned off all our office equipment. People were milling around, looking at desks and chairs and the bulky computers we used back then. I remember spotting someone I knew bidding on something, and I was mortified. It was so traumatic and heartbreaking to me. Even now, I could cry just thinking about it.

At the same time, I found that nothing spurs creativity quite like being flat broke. Having bills to pay and family members to support was a relentless motivator. My mind raced through all my options. What about swallowing my pride and applying for a job somewhere, just to get a little income going? I was willing. I was in agony and anything that would help was worth considering. But there was one big problem: I wasn't really qualified for anything! If this had been twenty years later, maybe I would have gone to work as an Uber driver, but Uber didn't exist then.

I did not want to go back to practicing law, but other than that, I had no easily transferable employment qualifications. I was actually afraid to apply for a job. Here I was, fifty years old, and my most recent work experience involved running a $50 million company that went broke. I couldn't stomach sitting through a job interview where I had to rehash all of that.

In the decades since then, I came to realize that failure is part of the process of maturing in business, and most employers and investors ascribe value to the experience. But at the time, I was beside myself. I needed a lightbulb to go off to show me the way forward. But the lightbulb in my head was on the blink. I was too addled by disappointment and desperation.

The more I thought about that lightbulb, I realized maybe there was something to that: a lightbulb on the blink. Faulty wiring. And for the first time in a decade, I started rethinking the details of home inspections.

I had long been fascinated by the power of new technology to transform the way whole sectors of business were run, and my work with American Home Shield gave me a close look at the world of home inspection. The new idea I had would, in a sense, make American Home Shield and I direct competitors, since at American Home Shield, we had offered clients a way to stop worrying so much about what home inspections turned up—or didn't.

"Why waste your money getting aggravated by a home inspection?" We would say. "We'll fix it if it's broken."

At one point while living in Northern California I had crossed paths with Larry Hoytt, who in 1976 had started a home inspection business in Novato, in nearby Marin County. Larry was active with the American Society of Home Inspectors, serving on the board and as legislative chairman. In March 1991, at a time when I needed a new idea in the worst way, I was flipping through the Sunday *San Francisco Examiner,* and spotted an item in Corrie Anders' real-estate column: "Lawrence A. Hoytt has been elected 1991 president of the Washington D.C.-based American Society of Home Inspectors."

So I called Larry and suggested we get together so I could pick his brain on the home-inspection business. He was amenable—amazing how often if you're kind, people are kind in return—but it took awhile to arrange. Eventually we met, and I was fascinated to learn about the home-inspection business from Larry. Here he was, almost my age, nine years younger, and he was still climbing around on rooftops and squeezing into crawl spaces to inspect houses. I asked him to walk me through the whole process and go over everything he did. He explained that as he inspected a house, he would take detailed notes, and then when he got back into the office he typed all the information into a word processor, cutting and pasting using his word-processing software. It sounded like a very inefficient process. He said he was only able to do one or two home inspections a day, in part because of the time he spent typing in the information afterward.

I met with realtors and asked them for their takes on the state of the home-inspection business. The joke—and I heard it a lot—was: *If you're a contractor and you hurt your back, then you buy a pickup truck, a ladder, and a Labrador retriever and go into the home-inspection business.* It was a great transition: You could charge three or four hundred bucks per inspection and you didn't need any special training or licensing. And best of all, you didn't have to do any heavy lifting!

"It's terrible," realtors kept telling me. "These guys are unreliable. They're undisciplined. They take no responsibility for their mistakes, and there are no standards. They don't even have to be licensed! They show up to inspect a house, and they're smart, but they think they're the smartest guys in the world," realtors complained. "Half the time, they kill the deal because they alarm the buyer about something that shouldn't be that alarming. And they often miss the things that *should* be alarming."

The business was simply not set up in a way to address the needs of realtors, or their homebuyers. The reports themselves were a crapshoot, and every home inspector had their own approach. Some wrote narrative reports and some offered checklists. Some included pictures, and others did not. Some organized their reports room by room—living room to dining room to kitchen to master bedroom, and so on—and others went system by system, plumbing and air-conditioning to electrical wiring to heating. The organization was confusing, and often so was the language. Even realtors often had difficulty understanding a home-inspection report. And if they wanted to get clarification later on, fat chance.

"When something goes wrong," realtors told me, "home inspectors make excuses or show you the fine print in their contract. Or even skip town. They never stand behind their product."

I knew that people like to complain. Some of what I heard was surely exaggeration. But it added up to a clear pattern that made me think there had to be a better way. **There was a need for innovation, that much was clear, and a market for any real innovation that could introduce better processes and a better business model.**

I decided it was worth doing more research.

In 1991, the American Society of Home Inspectors held its 14th annual Education Conference in nearby Phoenix, Arizona. I made plans to attend. These gatherings offered a fascinating window into the industry, partly educational, and partly a space for suppliers to hawk their wares. If you wanted to attend seminars on home construction or environmental concerns, or you were curious about the latest in state-of-the-art ladders or flashlights for home inspections, this was the place.

These conferences provided me with a quick study of an entire industry, between the educational sessions, the exhibition booths, and meeting and talking to practitioners, vendors, suppliers, consultants, and others on the periphery of the industry. I felt like a cultural anthropologist walking around, taking it all in.

The talks I attended at the convention in Phoenix were far more interesting than I expected, especially one hosting a panel of lawyers. The topic: How to avoid liability. That sounded reasonable enough, at first glance. Who doesn't want to avoid liability? But as a former attorney, I thought it through: Translated into real language, this was a panel on how to screw the customer. Because if you make a mistake on something important as a home inspector and are liable, you should pay for it. Otherwise, that expense is unjustly passed on to the customer.

I was amazed at how open and brazen the people at the convention were about trying to stick it to the unsuspecting innocents who trusted them to inspect their houses honorably and professionally! Doing so did not feel right. I had compassion; I was a homeowner myself.

At the end of the day, I left feeling that I could bring integrity to the business. **Moreover, I could apply quality training, standardized inspection, and responsible and updated business practices—including computers—to transform the home-inspection industry.** I just knew it. This was a question of when, not if, and I was sure I could make it happen. I knew that computers could clean up many of the problems I was seeing. I reasoned that with a little ingenuity and innovation, the right gadget powered by the right software might just revolutionize the industry. Where before there was rampant inconsistency and unreliable idiosyncrasies, we could create a consistent reporting system based on a standardized inspection that could be relied upon for its thoroughness, every time.

I got excited thinking about it. We should be able to come up with a program where the computer would prompt the inspector step-by-step on the inspection process. As each item was covered, the inspector would check the appropriate comment, then move on. For example, the program would include every conceivable comment an inspector might have on a ceiling fan: Check that box or boxes, and move on.

When the inspection was complete, instead of hours of studying notes and typing out whatever sort of report one wanted, a report was one push of a button away, and it would be compiled in a crisp, clear format that was the same for every report. All the plumbing would be listed room by room, then everything electrical, and so on. The language would be descriptive and helpful, but appropriate, not alarmist or Pollyannaish.

If our new system was created and it turned out to be as reliably consistent as I expected, then I was confident I could persuade an insurance company to insure every home inspection. This way, if mistakes were made, we would actually step up to the plate and pay for them!

Out of my failure with CompuFund came a creative, innovative idea. Perhaps if I hadn't sat with my failure, and instead had taken any old job, I would have never opened the door for my next venture. Some people see failure as the end, and they cannot move beyond it. Thankfully, I saw failure as an opportunity and finally understood how important it was to success.

CHAPTER 10

Mastering the Formula with Inspectech

As I mentioned previously, Bob Giles, our former director of Management Information Systems at American Home Shield, had been an ex-cop from Chicago. There must have been something about ex-cops that primed them for computer programming because in 1992, I met a former California Highway Patrol officer named Hal Spice who also had a knack for technology. Hal was a very kind, quiet, and engaging guy who was great at software development.

That was the real beginning of Inspectech. Hal Spice drove every day from Stockton to our home in Alamo to work on this program. I gave him my ideas on how it should work, and he set about creating the actual program. In order to write the encyclopedia on home inspections, we needed to do extensive research on exactly what home inspectors were inspecting, and what they could possibly say about what was being inspected.

We knew we needed help to do this research, and I was thankful when my daughter Gabby and a friend of hers from high school, Todd, offered to help. Gabby graduated from College Preparatory School in Oakland in 1991 before attending UCLA. She and Todd did an incredible job. They pored over books on home inspection to cover as much ground as possible and then interviewed home inspectors at length. They asked these inspectors about everything they could think of and took notes on their replies, compiling as many potential answers as they could to every question on their list, getting the full rundown on the details of each item on the inspection list. It turned out there were several hundred individual items that needed attention.

"OK, if you're looking at a gas-fired heating system, what do you look for?" They might ask.

Or: "What are the warning signs that an air-conditioning unit might be on its last legs?"

I brought together a half-dozen local home inspectors to serve as advisors to help build the "encyclopedia" of home inspections, and to help Gabby prepare the thousands of comments that might be used to describe what an inspector saw. This part of the process was always interesting. At times we would be talking to two home inspectors and they would get so worked up over a difference in opinion, I thought someone was going to swing a lug wrench at someone's head. These were debates over topics like whether to call something a faucet or a valve.

"No, it's not a faucet," one would say in a brook-no-opposition tone of voice.

"No, it's not a valve," the other would say, even more set in his thinking.

"Come on, Larry, you've got to call it a faucet, not a valve," one would say.

"Absolutely not—if it turns this way, it's a valve," Larry would argue.

It was the kind of thing that made me crazy.

But Gabby compiled and typed out thousands of these potential descriptions on every conceivable component in a home—a total of more than 12,500 comments that amounted to a veritable encyclopedia of home inspection. We gave all that information to Hal Spice for the computer program he was developing. He would do little demonstrations of what he was working on every so often, showing me the way it looked on his screen, and it all seemed great to me. We were making progress. If only we could keep all this going on a shoestring. It was an outstanding program, a true game-changer.

Our development phase was not the most traditional, but this is the way you get a business started: **Flesh out the vision. Talk to a lot of people who know what they're doing. Figure out what has to be done and what human and cash resources you need to do it. Write up a plan of action. Get to work. And never give up.**

I always loved talking about what our system could do, and I knew it was the wave of the future. "This is becoming the key to our home inspections," I told the *Modesto Bee* in 1997. "Guiding the inspector each step of the way, this state-of-the-art device prompts the inspector with a list of every potential condition in the home—up to 8,000 specific conditions. It even covers such things as a leaky water heater and incorrect spacing of shingles on the roof. Ultimately, it's the quality of the home inspection and resulting report that will dictate our level of success in the view of consumers. Our research team spent three years and over $1 million to create this system."

I still had a lot to learn about the home-inspection business, so I asked Larry Hoytt to join our board. It seemed to be the right move. Larry helped me think through how to turn this idea into a real business, and he introduced me to other home inspectors who could potentially work for us or just give advice. Like most people in the home-inspection business, Larry and his friends tended to have high opinions of their own insights. It took some work to keep them focused and working harmoniously with each other.

Through it all, I was flat broke, barely covering the mortgage on our home. Somehow I came up with enough to pay Hal something for his work, though not all I owed him.

After a year, we'd done it. We had a finished product, but I had no resources to take it forward. I'd already been borrowing whatever I could, maxing out credit cards, kiting checks, you name it. I was not in a position to ask too many hard questions if someone turned up willing to invest, and that ended up being a very painful lesson for me in what *not* to do in business. In fact, I hate thinking about this period of my life.

My vision had always been that our program—which we called Wizard 2000—would be used on small, portable tablet computers we'd supply to home inspectors. With the help of an investor, who put up some funds in exchange for stock in the company, we were able to finish the program and launch the company. It was so good, we were wowing people with our program.

We made a purchase of GRiDPad tablet computers, which were very new then, introduced in 1989 as the first consumer-focused tablet device, even before the Palm Pilot. The product, as a *New York Times* article in 1989 explained, "was not aimed at replacing paper or other portable computers, but at providing a more accurate and accessible way to enter data from the field." Exactly.

Developed by a company in nearby Fremont, California, Grid Systems Corp., this was a precursor to the iPad with a tethered electronic pen that you touched to the screen to write. They were an inch and a half thick, about the size of a clipboard. Even the U.S. Army was starting to use them. I bought a few dozen ruggedized GRiD-Pad tablets and showed them to Hal Spice. He came back to me a day or two later with bad news.

"It's not going to work," he said. "We need six MEGs of memory capacity to run the program, and the GRiDPad doesn't have nearly enough."

"There has to be a way, Hal. Take another look," I pleaded with him.

Hal took another look.

"It won't work," he told me again. "You'll have to equip home inspectors with a full desktop computer they set up at each house."

Full desktop computer! It was a nightmare! My vision was all about simplicity and ease transforming the industry. I couldn't imagine trying to convince hordes of surly home inspectors to set up a full desktop computer every time they arrived at a new house. I was beside myself. We had come so far, but it looked like the whole business was already unraveling.

I owed Hal money, I was out of people I could ask for a loan, and I had a roomful of tablet computers that were apparently useless to us.

So I asked for help. Again, if you're genuine, if you ask the right way, it's amazing how often people will try to help deliver you from the hell you've entered. I was fortunate to have a friend, George Turin, who might have useful suggestions. George was chairman of the UC Berkeley Department of Electrical Engineering and Computer Science in the 1980s, and in 1983 took over for a few years as dean of the UCLA School of Engineering and Applied Sciences, before coming back to Berkeley. And he was a great friend of Susan's and mine. I met with George, explained my problems, and asked if he could help.

"I can't help you," he said, "but I might know someone who can. Limin Hu was the smartest student I've ever had; he was in my graduate program."

Limin wrote his PhD dissertation, with George as his advisor, on "Electrostatic Comb Drive for Resonant Sensor and Actuator Applications." Too smart for me!

"If he can't figure this out, nobody can," George said.

So I called Limin and laid out the problem, asking for his help. He said he thought he could find a solution.

"There's only one problem," I said. "I can't pay you."

There was silence on the phone.

"But what I'll do," I said, "because I'm sure this is going to be a winner, and I think we're going to take over the world with home inspections, is this: I can agree to pay you $100,000. But it will be one dollar per inspection. Every time we do an inspection, we'll pay you $1."

"Fine," he said. He wasn't thrilled, but he was intrigued.

Within two weeks, Limin had solved the problem. He figured out a way to compress some of the files to make the software compatible with the GRiDPad.

We were off and running, and we had a fabulous product—a show stopper. The best part was the ease: Inspectors walked through a house, using the device at every stop, and when they finished they simply plugged the GRiDPad into a printer and voila, a full report came out in no time.

Everyone loved us! It was such an easy sell, explaining to realtors that we would charge $100 or so more than for other inspections, but ours would be much better—and they knew we were right. The realtor didn't mind paying a little extra for a more reliable inspection, which was also insured, since the consumer paid for it anyway, and it was good for business all around. My pitch tended to go over very well with realtors.

"Look, there's a perfect inspection," I would say. "It's written in the King's English. It's not going to spook your customer. It's going to cover your customer. And if we make a mistake, we'll pay for it."

That was probably enough to hook them, most of the time, but then I followed up with transcripts of seminars where home inspectors were taught how to avoid having to pay liability claims.

"Is this true?" they would say.

"It's true," I would say. "You can go to the convention yourself next time. You can see HOW TO AVOID CLAIMS right there on the agenda. Who do you want to deal with: somebody who stands behind their product or some guy in a pickup truck who doesn't have a license—and doesn't take responsibility for mistakes?"

We were doing well and kept adding inspectors. We actually couldn't find enough to do the work! So I figured we could start training new home inspectors. In February 1992, we published classified ads in the *San Francisco Examiner* looking for full-time or part-time home inspectors, "Exp. not nec. Contractor's lic. pref'd. Send resumes to Inspectech Corp, 2496 Royal Oaks Drive in Alamo, California."

In June 1992, the *Examiner* published an article on us, explaining that Inspectech Corp., "an Alamo company that provides computerized home inspections, has appointed three veteran inspectors as regional directors": Larry Hoytt, for the North Bay region, Doug Hanson for the South Bay, and Greg Marell for the East Bay.

"Sig Anderman, fifty, Inspectech's chief executive, said the firm guarantees to deliver inspection reports within twenty-four hours or provide them without cost. Non-computerized reports often take several days for preparation and delivery," the *Examiner* article added.

We hit the market in early 1993 and we kept growing, but we were having problems with cash flow. We ended up with a couple hundred inspectors, and some months cash flow was positive, but some months it wasn't. The investor who I'd brought in early on turned out to be a royal pain in the ass. Every week or two we would have a meeting, and I would have to listen to an earful from him, basically just nagging me and making noise: "Why don't you have this?" or "Collect on these receivables!" or "Charge more for your services!" or "Charge less for your services!"

It was making me crazy. We had a great product, but we did not yet have a great business model or a great strategy. I knew I needed more time to come up with something. **That's how startups evolve: Trial and error. Track progress. Understand what's working and what's not. Keep tweaking the product until you get it right.** But my investor gave me no room to breathe. No maneuverability. And that's exactly what you need when starting a new business, because nothing ever, ever works or rolls out the way you planned. **You have to keep listening, keep measuring, and keep adjusting, sometimes dramatically.** And if you can't do that, you almost always run into brick walls—sometimes too late to correct the business model.

To add to the stress, I ended up expanding too fast—way before I had perfected the business model. That was a classic startup mistake, and I learned my lesson the hard way.

I was back in New York for a wedding and decided to do some market research in my spare time. I called up Jim Weichert, founder of Weichert Realtors, who I knew from my American Home Shield days. Weichert was one of the top residential real-estate operations in the country, with more than 9,000 real-estate agents at that point—at least one magazine had named Weichert the No. 1 agency in the country. I told Jim I was on the East Coast and we should get together for lunch. I drove to Morris Plains, New Jersey, to see him and asked him what he thought about our amazing home-inspection tool.

"You think your agents would like it?" I asked.

"Like it?" Jim said. "They'd love it."

He was serious.

"When can you start?" he asked me.

He caught me totally by surprise. I wasn't planning on that quick a close.

"Give me six months to hire inspectors," I said.

So I got to work hiring home inspectors on the East Coast, in New Jersey and later New Hampshire and Massachusetts, where Weichert also had offices. By then I should have been having fun with this business, but everything was much harder than it should have been. We had a good automation system, and a good team, but we needed time—and money—to get the model right.

But I had an investor who was a major pain, who was unwilling to invest their $2 million commitment to us up front. In the scheme of things, $2 million is not that much to transform a multi-billion-dollar industry, and to create a hundred-or-so-million-dollar company. And each month, I would literally have to beg them for funds. This meant that I could never plan ahead, and I had no room to figure things out. No space for trial and error. I was, in hindsight, doomed to fail.

What's more, the home inspectors themselves were making me crazy. I had to baby-sit them every day, it often seemed. The beauty of the system was that our device standardized the format of both inspections and reports, and the inspectors didn't have to sweat all the details—but they did anyway.

I'd get calls from inspectors telling me they thought the report should be landscape-oriented rather than portrait. Or telling me we had to start using color photographs, instead of black and white. Or telling me we needed to make a change in how we referred to air-conditioning systems. I was tired of hearing it. The situation grew really unpleasant for me.

I learned a few lessons from the Inspectech experience. **First, don't expand before you're ready. Really ready. More companies die of**

indigestion—growing too fast—than starvation! I also learned how to handle investors. I wasn't smart enough then. I kept going back to our investors and asking for more money, but I'd ask for just enough to get by. I felt awkward asking for more. **I learned later that you have to ask for enough money to give yourself some breathing room.** I needed to ask for another million, not $50,000 at a time to make that week's payroll and then immediately start worrying about the next week.

You can't live that way. It exhausts you. It eats you up. You have to be kinder to yourself than that.

After four years, the board ended up going behind my back to hire a president under me, which undermined me. Worse, he wasn't even qualified and only made my life harder. So I finally had to throw in the towel. It was terrible. I thought to myself: *Shit, I'm fifty-six years old, and I don't like this any more.* So in 1998, I told the investors to buy me out and take over the company. It was too stressful to continue, and they decided it was time for them to jump ship as well, so they sold the company.

The technology and the product were great; we should have had a winning business, but our investors never gave me the latitude or the running room to make it work, and I let myself get tripped up by that. I knew that was a mistake I could never make again. I'd have to bring a different attitude to any other businesses I was going to start.

CHAPTER 11

What's Fate Got to Do With It?

The whole thing was a nightmare. It was 1997. I was fifty-six years old and broke. Our credit cards were maxed out—once again. We had a big house and a mortgage we weren't sure we could cover. We had school bills to pay for our son and daughters, and a dozen other financial headaches. I was under so much pressure after the bizarre collapse of CompuFund—a business I'd started and built up into a thriving concern—losing it just as it was about to set us up for life. And then Inspectech was a bust. I was reeling.

But through it all, Susan and I were still going to the symphony. Nothing could take that away from us. It was important to Susan, my wife of thirty-three years at that point, and that made it important to me. We were going, no matter how gloomy I felt. That was that.

Usually when we attended a performance at Davies Symphony Hall in San Francisco, we knew just where our seats were. That was part of what we loved about being season ticket holders. Susan always chose the "keyboard" side of the orchestra section, just to the left of the center aisle, with a direct view of the piano soloist, if there was one, and of the conductor, arms raised to the music. We knew we'd be surrounded by the familiar faces of other season ticket holders we'd been seeing for years. But not this time. One performance, we were assigned new seats after a rescheduled show; that placement, it turned out, changed our lives.

We found our row just as the first violinist started off with an A, and the strings and all the woodwinds tuned up to meet the violin. The conductor, Michael Tilson Thomas, would stride out any minute. As I took my seat, someone tapped me on the shoulder to say hello.

"Sig!" a voice said.

I looked over.

"It's Sig, from May Lake," the man explained to his girlfriend.

It was Barr Dolan, a man I had spoken to only once in my life before this night at the symphony. That was four years earlier, sitting around a campfire high in the mountains above Yosemite National Park. For years I had been dreaming of hiking from hut to hut in the High Sierras, and in 1996, I finally did it. We turned it into a team-building getaway for my company, Inspectech, with fifty-something Sig and four thirty- to forty-year-olds clambering on rocky mountain paths. One of them, Barry Prentice, our Colorado manager, had climbed every peak above 10,000 feet in the Rockies. I was the only novice!

The twist was, we didn't have to lug around tents or food or big puffy sleeping bags. That was all taken care of for us through the High Sierra Camps. You carried a light pack with a few snacks and water, maybe extra sunscreen, and showed up at your destination. They served you meals prepared by chefs doing internships at the Culinary Institute in San Francisco, with ingredients brought in on the backs of mules. And they put you up in real tents with real bathrooms and showers.

It was an exhilarating experience, my ankles somehow survived, and up there at Camp May Lake, I met Barr for the first time.

He was a hiker who just randomly sat next to me on a log in front of a campfire. We spoke mainly about our hiking over the previous couple days, and where we were going next. Toward the end of the evening, we talked about what we did when we weren't hiking. Barr told me he was a venture capitalist.

"Sig, the next time you start something, give me a call," he said up in the mountains.

I said I would.

"I'm serious," he added.

Barr was an interesting fellow. He'd earned an undergraduate degree at Stanford in engineering and applied sciences, and then added an MBA in 1976. He'd specialized in investing in early technology and medical companies, and done very well. And I could tell that, like me, he enjoyed getting to know people and cultivating relationships in a genuine way. He was tough, but a very kind, honest, and decent human being. He got where he was by making good decisions; he was a critical thinker who did not suffer fools or bullshit. He had the track record of success to trust his hunches, and he'd had a hunch about me.

Now Barr was sitting right next to me at the symphony, which was divine providence of some sort. The only problem was the house lights had just dimmed, and we couldn't talk right then. I was left to take in the music and think about my predicament. At least Susan was happy. Far from settling my thoughts, the crescendo of the first and second movements unleashed them. I kept coming back to an idea I'd had for another business startup, a simple concept that used the newly developed Internet to make it a lot easier for people to get home mortgages.

Barr and I did not have a chance to talk that night at the symphony. He left during the intermission.

"Let's get lunch," he said on his way out.

"Fantastic," I said.

At lunch with Barr the next week, I laid out my mortgage software company idea for him, and he listened intently. Why did it have to be so complicated to get a mortgage? So aggravating? So time-consuming? My vision from the beginning was that we would find a way to do a mortgage for you in forty-five minutes—maybe even forty-five seconds—instead of forty-five days. Everything was speeding up to the pace of the Internet, so why not?

"I don't know how the Internet works," I told Barr, "but I have a hunch we can figure out how to do a mortgage in forty-five minutes. We'll just connect electronically to all the people, all the data, all the documents you need to approve a mortgage—credit report, title report, appraisal, income, and asset and liability information, and get it all in seconds."

"I'm in," he said.

"You're in?" I said.

"Five hundred thousand," he said. "I can give you $500,000 to get going."

"What's the catch?" I asked, smiling. "There's got to be a catch. What do you get out of it?"

"I'll take 20 percent of the company," he said.

"That's it?" I asked. "You put up the money and get just 20 percent?"

"I'm good with 20," he said.

"But do you understand I know nothing about the Internet or how it works, it's only a hunch I have?" I asked.

"That's what I do, I bet on hunches," Barr replied.

I really couldn't believe my good luck, but I wasn't going to waste time thinking about it: I had a company to build!

"It's a deal," I said, "why don't you send me the paperwork?"

Within a week, Barr sent me a two-page document, perfectly describing what we had agreed to.

Now I felt like the dog chasing the school bus: What do you do when you catch it? I caught it, but I had no idea how to automate the mortgage process!

The first guy I called was Limin Hu, the man I had used as a consultant in my home inspection business, after my friend George Turin of UC Berkeley recommended him to me. I knew Limin was a genius. He didn't know a mortgage from a motor boat, but that was okay. Actually, it was better than okay.

Initially, I only hired people who had no knowledge whatsoever of the mortgage business, none at all. This was by design, not an accident. No one in the mortgage business believed it could be automated, instead asserting, "It's more art than science." **I'd heard enough naysayers. I'd gotten a belly full of pessimism. I wanted people with a can-do attitude, no matter what their backgrounds.**

"We're going to do a forty-five minute mortgage!" I told Limin.

"Great," he said. "Let's go!" He didn't know enough to be intimidated.

The head of product I eventually hired to do the hard work of designing this new product, Jonathan Corr, was as much of a neophyte in this area as the tech guy. The closest he had ever come to a mortgage was getting one.

But sometimes expertise and industry experience lead to learning bad habits and blinding yourself. If you came fresh to the question of getting a mortgage back in that era, you had to scratch your head and ask, "Why is it so cumbersome? Isn't there a better way?" Even then, you could walk into a village in Estonia or Ecuador, pull out your ATM card, and get money in twenty seconds. No one needed to know you. No one vetted you to see if you were a fraud. It was just: Stick in the card and—bing!—twenty seconds later you could get $500. Why, you could even get a $25,000 car loan in an hour. But for a mortgage, it had to take forty-five days? Sixty days? Even longer? It just didn't make any sense that it was so slow.

Later, as we built the company, we obviously had to hire people that had been in the business, but I was in no hurry. **My first hires, the ones who created the product and programmed the first software, they were like blank slates who looked to me and took me at my word when I said this could be done. I needed to be surrounded by wide-open optimism, like what I felt from Barr when I told him my idea at that lunch.**

Years later, Barr told me the real story on why he'd invested. Spoiler alert: It was not a question of him being wowed by my idea.

"I knew you didn't know what you were talking about, but I liked you. I trusted you and I knew you'd figure it out someday," he explained.

That was the way he worked. **Most investors, I learned later, just invest in people. They put their faith in people they think are smart, honest, and determined enough to make their ideas a reality.** Barr knew that I was, but he also invested in me because we made a connection rooted in kindness and camaraderie on that hiking trip. He remained my partner and an investor for twenty years until we sold the company for $3.7 billion dollars. That was twenty years after we met on a log at May Lake. What a hiking trip. And that's what fate has to do with it!

CHAPTER 12

What's in a Name?

The real start of my billion-dollar company that Barr divinely invested in began on Thanksgiving of 1998. Thanksgiving was always a highlight for our family. We like to eat, get together, and catch up, so what's not to like about an annual feast? We didn't sing old Bob Dylan songs the way we did for Passover, where we used our own version of the Haggadah, but Thanksgiving was a day we all looked forward to. Susan was a great cook and so were my children, Elissa, David, and Gabby. Everyone cooked their favorite dish, and the meal was always fabulous. I remember our mood being especially upbeat for the holiday in 1998. Months earlier, I'd been fighting just to keep afloat, but with the new business idea underway, things were looking up.

Elissa, our oldest, turned thirty-three that year, David was twenty-nine, and Gabby was twenty-seven. They were old enough to have long since cleared childhood, and all three had their own lives going on. It was fun to have some developments of my own to share with them.

"I'm starting a new company," I announced at one point.

This announcement earned a round of smiles, but it wasn't as if this was the first time I had started a new company.

"We're going to revolutionize the mortgage industry!" I continued. "With our software, we're going to automate the whole process of getting a mortgage. And use the Internet to find borrowers and process and fund a loan in days, maybe minutes, instead of weeks or months."

I was beaming.

"That sounds great, Dad!" they said, excited for me, but maybe not quite as excited as I was.

"What's the name of the company?" David asked.

"Electronic Mortgage Affiliates," I told them. "All the businesses involved in processing a mortgage will be connected—affiliated—using the Internet. Banks, credit bureaus, title companies, appraisers. Everyone."

They stared at me. Looks were exchanged. I'd learned by then that by the time your kids get to be in their twenties and thirties, they love to carry on just knowing they are smarter than you are, and wondering how you ever got as far as you did in life.

"Electronic Mortgage Affiliates?" David said slowly, his eyebrows rising. "That's the name? You're serious?"

"Absolutely!" I said.

He shook his head.

"Dad, that's a stupid name," he said. "It's so 1960s."

"Oh really?" I said quickly, bristling a little. "Well if you're so smart, come up with a better name."

David was amused. So were Susan, Elissa, and Gabby.

"You want us to name your company?" David asked.

"Sure, have at it," I said, trying to sound grumpy, but we were all having too much fun.

It was as if I'd come up with some new party game for the holiday. Instead of charades or Trivial Pursuits, we'd play "Name Dad's new company." David didn't need much time to think.

"Why don't we make it sound like Fannie Mae and Freddie Mac?" he suggested. "If you have a mortgage company, it should be one of those."

Fannie Mae is the name everyone uses for the Federal National Mortgage Association. Freddie Mac is the Federal Home Loan Mortgage Corporation.

David brainstormed for all of two or three minutes before it came to him.

"How about shortening Electronic Mortgage Affiliates?" he suggested. "Maybe an acronym?"

I liked where he was going.

"How about Ellie Mae?" he said.

"That's perfect!" Gabby said, and everyone agreed. "That other name was so boring. It didn't do anything. Ellie Mae! I like it."

I loved it, too! Smiles and nods spread around the room. It was a good name.

And if you're wondering, David has always explained that although he watched plenty of *The Beverly Hillbillies* growing up, he was not thinking of Elly May, Jethro, Jed, and Granny when he made the suggestion. "It must have been subconscious," he says.

Ellie Mae was actually a brilliant choice. It made everyone think of Fannie Mae, which in 1998 was the premier company in the mortgage industry and one of the most admired companies in the world. When people thought of Fannie Mae, they thought of making homes affordable—and making money for shareholders. It had been formed sixty years earlier. As *Time Magazine* explained, "During the Great Depression, as borrowers defaulted on mortgages en masse and banks found themselves strapped for cash, President Franklin D. Roosevelt and Congress created Fannie Mae in 1938 in order to buy mortgages from lenders, freeing up capital that could go to other borrowers."

The more I thought about the name David had suggested, the more I wondered if it was too good to be true.

"I wonder if it's available," I said.

"I can check," he said, and he picked up the phone in the house (a land line, which was what we used back then) and made a call.

David worked as an intellectual property lawyer, and knew just who to call to check the necessary databases. He talked to someone briefly, then waited to see what their search turned up.

"Pops, it's available!" he called out to me after a while. "Do you want it?"

I couldn't believe he had an answer for me, just like that.

"Yeah, get it," I said.

"It's fifteen bucks," he said. "Give me your credit card."

We trademarked the name, changed our corporate name, and did our best to move on, but I still worried. It all felt too easy. Something had to go wrong. I was really concerned that Fannie Mae would object to my using a name that could be confused with theirs. That, of course, was my intention! But I didn't want to get sued.

Within days after we started using the new name, an article appeared in major industry publications, *American Banker* and *National Mortgage News*, telling the mortgage community about the launch of Ellie Mae. I waited for the phone to ring—expecting a call from some attorney in Washington demanding that I change the name. But no calls came.

A year went by. We kept improving our software, and trying to figure out the right model for our business. First we tried to function as a lender and just use the software ourselves to make loans. That didn't quite click, and we changed the strategy to license the software to established mortgage brokers and small mortgage lenders. Bingo. We had found the right approach.

All the while, I thought it was just a matter of time before

Fannie Mae complained. Time, though, was on our side. The law on potential trademark infringement was straightforward. If anyone thought there were grounds to sue you for infringing on a trademarked name, they would have to object within one year from the time they became aware of your name or should have become aware. After one year transpired, if they had lodged no complaint, they were barred from objecting. We'd be in the clear. No going back.

In the meantime, we kept busy selling our software. We reached out to people in the industry all over the country and gave our pitch that the time frame on getting a mortgage could be reduced from forty-five days to four or five. And the cost of processing a loan could be reduced dramatically. I would fly around the country and we would rent a hotel room and bring in twenty to thirty mortgage brokers at a time. Our software was cheap, relatively speaking, and most brokers immediately saw the advantages. We were steadily adding clients, month by month, and approaching the one-year deadline by which any complaints would have to be registered. I was still a little tense about the name.

Two weeks before we hit the one-year mark, I got a call from Fannie Mae. Really? At the eleventh hour? They'd clearly been playing a game of cat and mouse with us, and we both knew who was the cat and who was the mouse.

"We're doing an analysis of all the mortgage software out there," Tom Booker from Fannie Mae told me. "You're on our radar. We want to figure out what software we want to adopt or promote."

I told him that sounded great. What else was I going to say? I was in no position to call anyone's bluff.

"We'd like to come down and meet you," he added.

I was two weeks away from making it through the year with no challenge to our company name.

"Sure," I said. "Let me check my calendar."

I paused for a minute as if I was checking the calendar.

"Hmm, looks like the next two weeks are not good," I said. "In fact, the next three weeks I'm tied up. How about after that?"

They told me that would be fine. Again, too easy. I hung up and immediately called my son David, to ask about any exceptions to the one-year rule. He couldn't think of any, he said, but that didn't settle the issue for me. I was sure I knew what I'd hear from the Fannie Mae group that came to see me.

I started practicing what to say when they confronted me.

"Listen, I'm so sorry I used that name," I tried saying. "How much do I have to pay you?"

No, no, that was no good.

"There's plenty of room for everybody in this business," I practiced. "It's not going to be that confusing. Fannie Mae is not Ellie Mae!"

I rehearsed that one with real feeling, but felt like I was practicing a belly-flop off the high dive. This was not going to be pretty.

Finally, the day of their visit arrived. I met four or five guys from Fannie Mae, led by Tom Booker, a big, strapping corporate executive, carrying a massive brown briefcase. I shook all their hands, greeted them, and tried to figure out who in the group was the attorney who would be suing me. I suspected the summons would be in Tom's briefcase.

"We'd like to see a demo of the software," they told me.

Sure, sure, we could do that. We had it all ready. But what was this, Kabuki theater? We had no idea. I tried to stay cool as they watched the demo and then started talking about how impressed they were. This was some game of cat and mouse! I had no idea where they were going with this.

Finally they left—without suing. A few weeks later, they

followed up.

Tom called me. "You've got the best software out there," he told me. "And we want to endorse it."

Which they did. They were such fans, in fact, that I reached out to them a few months later to see if they might want to invest. Tom was interested. I flew to Washington to meet with his team. They agreed to invest $5 million, and lead an investment round of $28 million that included First American Title, General Electric, and PMI—the same PMI, led by Preston Martin, that had helped me with the CompuFund concept.

But it was all contingent on getting Fannie Mae to lead the round. I had to get that done, but it was not as easy as the investment by Barr a few years earlier. It took six months to pin them down on the particulars. I called Tom Booker at Fannie Mae every day or two to check in on when we could finally close the deal. Deadlines for finalizing the documents would come and go. He always had some explanation for the delays. It got down to me calling him at home, sometimes a couple times a day—during breakfast, or dinner, when I knew he would have a free moment. Just when I thought he would drag it out forever, we finally got it all wrapped up.

"We'll wire you the funds," Tom told me.

"No," I said, "I don't want a wire. I'm still old fashioned. I want to see a check."

I flew to Washington to pick up the check for $5,000,000 directly from Mike Williams, the president of Fannie Mae—to hold it up and take a long, hard look. I went up in front of the group to accept the check from the president. Everybody applauded, shook hands, and applauded some more.

"From the first time we saw an article about your company, we were impressed with you and what you were doing," Mike said. "But we didn't know whether to sue you or invest in you—I'm glad we decided to invest."

So were we. And it worked out well for everyone. They bought stock at about two dollars per share, which they could later sell for more than fifty times that price. I'd call that a nice return on investment. The same was true for other investors in that round, who together with Fannie Mae invested a total of $28 million in our company. And got back close to $2 billion.

CHAPTER 13

Easy Living in the Not-Exactly-a-Commune

As a kid growing up in New York City, I always dreamed of one day having a place in the country with grass, trees, and maybe even a lake or a stream running through it. My life then was circumscribed by West 16th Street in Chelsea, and a few blocks in each direction. There were no trees to be seen. Occasionally, gray "Play Street" police barriers would be set up at each end of the street, so no cars could enter. That meant the street was our playground for the day. Like city kids everywhere, we improvised games—running bases, stoop ball sometimes, but mainly stick ball. One manhole cover, which we called a "sewer," would be first base, and another would be second base. A fire hydrant—we called it a "pump"—would be third base, and we'd figure out something for home plate.

I loved it, but always wished I was somewhere else. I'd be in the middle of a stickball game, concrete and macadam all around me, and I'd think: Someday I'd love to have a ranch, maybe something like the Ponderosa Ranch on the TV program *Bonanza*, which I was dreaming of long before it premiered on television when I was seventeen.

I never stopped thinking of that vision of living on a ranch somewhere. It was an idea that tugged at my imagination, and my wife Susan shared my curiosity about a life like that—with horses, a little pond with a rowboat and a dock for fishing, a great climate for a robust vegetable garden, the works. We wanted nature on all sides, and we wanted raw beauty, but other than that, we were flexible.

So when we came to a place in our lives where we could actually afford to consider looking for a ranch we could call home—about fifteen years after we moved to California—we cast a wide net. Our search began in the mid-1990s when I was still working at the Inspectech headquarters in the East Bay, near San Francisco. We were renting our apartment in the city, and wanted a second spot no more than a three-hour drive away. We drove north, we drove south, and we drove east; we looked down along Monterey Bay, near Santa Cruz and other beach communities, and we drove all the way up to potential properties near Yosemite and in Willits along the Mendocino National Forest.

We were, in a sense, budget shopping. We were in no position to drop millions on a second home, but the only options we found were exactly that much, often coming with sizable plots of land. We found some attractive places that were affordable, but too far away to get to, even if just on weekends. We also had countless disappointing experiences of driving down some country road, trying to stay optimistic, and yet again showing up to find the "ranch" we were hoping to see was in fact yet another example of a "ranch house." That's not at all the same thing. I can't tell you how many realtors we talked to who did not understand the distinction.

"I have this great ranch house for you!" we'd be told.

No! We didn't want a ranch-style house on half an acre. We wanted to feel like we were on the set of *Bonanza*!

Finally, in 1998, not long after I founded Ellie Mae, we met a realtor couple in Sonoma who listened and understood. It was a great feeling to finally resonate with someone who shared our vision—when this realtor called, it was different.

"Sig, I've got a great property to show you," they said one day. "It's about a hundred acres. It has a four-acre pond with two row boats and a swimming dock. It's pretty good for fishing. A stream runs alongside the property, and it also has a barn, as well as an organic garden and organic orchards."

It sounded great. It sounded perfect, almost too perfect.

"And it's in Forestville, only an hour and fifteen minute drive from San Francisco," they continued.

I was stunned hearing all of this. There had to be a catch. What was the catch?

"What's the price?" I asked.

"Three hundred and fifty thousand," the realtor said.

"What?" I said. "Am I hearing you right? Did you really say $350,000?"

"Yes, I did," he said. "It's a great price. But it's not for everybody."

He explained that we'd be buying into an unusual community: Thomas Creek Ranch. There were eleven homeowners who each individually owned a lot of an acre or so, maybe half an acre. There were more than ninety acres held jointly, and it was prime land, taking up a small valley, with a large pasture area, beautiful vegetable and flower gardens, white fences, and hiking trails. There was a swimming pool, sauna, hot tub, and a guest house, which all could use. Plus a flock of thirty chickens to lay fresh eggs.

"So it's a community and you have to get along," the realtor explained.

Thomas Creek Ranch had been founded in the early 1970s as a commune. Each family owned their own home and a small plot of land around it, but they shared everything else. The families gardened together, taught their children together, and cooked their meals and ate together. They even swam naked together—this was the early '70s in Northern California, after all. But the commune approach did not last long. It dissipated when all that contact with each other got on everyone's nerves. But there were still communal aspects, like a work session every other Saturday morning from 9 to 12, when the entire community would gather to handle an endless list of ranch chores—to clear brush, clean the chicken coop, repair bridges and hiking trails, mend fences, work in the gardens—whatever was needed. And once a month and on holidays, they would all have dinner together.

I found the history of the place intriguing. The founder of Thomas Creek Ranch was Louis Sloss Jr., who died in April 2019 at age ninety-six. His grandfather, Louis Sloss Sr., was born to a Jewish family in Bavaria and emigrated to the U.S. Louis Sr. made a fortune in post-Gold Rush California, operating a string of general merchandise stores and co-founding the Alaska Commercial Company. His grandson, Louis Jr., along with Louis Jr.'s wife, Jean-Elsa, joined three other families in founding the Thomas Creek Ranch as an "intentional community," inspired in part by Stanford Law professor Harry Rathbun's lectures on living a meaningful life.

Susan and I weren't sure what to think. We weren't commune people. We were from New York! But we wanted to take a look. We made the drive up to the Forestville area and drove down the mile-long, one-lane road leading to the property itself. It was breathtaking, exactly what I had been dreaming of all those years, with a barn and twenty-five-acre pasture bounded by a white fence.

The realtor knew just what he was doing. He started out his tour of the place by walking us along the beautiful lake, a deep, shimmering pond taking up almost four acres, a great spot for swimming and fishing or paddling around in a row boat. Again, exactly as I'd imagined. As soon as I saw that lake, I knew we were going to buy the house, no matter what it looked like. And as luck would have it, the house was just beautiful—a perfect second home for us.

We didn't meet the other homeowners until shortly before we closed on the house, which was right around Christmas, 1999. We gathered in the community center—with a kitchen and dining area—to meet everyone and let them ask us some questions.

"So what do you think of this community?" someone asked me.

"What do I *think*?" I said, my voice almost cracking. "It's what I've been dreaming about for fifty years. It's fabulous. I can't believe it."

That set the tone. We smiled at them, they smiled back—and we all got along beautifully right from the get-go. Susan and I both loved it up there. We were the only ones who did not live there full time. But for the next ten or fifteen years, Susan and I were up there almost every weekend.

It was no McMansion, not a fancy place at all—that was part of what we loved about it—but the whole community was laid out with extreme care. It was beautiful and understated. In fact, one of the founding families had paid to bring in famed landscape architect Thomas Church, trained at UC Berkeley and Harvard and the founder of the California Style, to design the homes. Church, a disciple of Central Park designer Frederick Law Olmsted, bucked the trend toward neoclassical design and favored a new approach that emphasized four elements: unity, function, simplicity, and scale.

And those qualities were all in abundance at Thomas Creek Ranch. It's no commune, but the commitment to intentional living—even if I'm not sure quite what that means, besides being truly kind—seems to have translated into a remarkable warmth and respect for one another. Fifty years after the founding, people live together who like each other, work together well and get along, obey the rules, and oversee thriving gardens and orchards.

Our time there also introduced me to a new passion: gardening. I loved the physicality of digging up soil and planting. I also loved the process of seeing a seed or a seedling take root, of planting string beans, tomatoes, dinosaur kale, or flowers, and watching them grow, through every stage of germination. I loved when a garden was growing. And I loved it when I was pulling everything out at the end of the season—in the early winter, late spring, and late fall. I especially loved eating what I'd grown and picked. I loved the distraction from everyday concerns. And I loved that this was a hobby with such nourishing results. With most things in life, it's hard to see results so quickly. But within six months of planting a seed, I could see the fruits of my labor.

Susan and I realized soon after we moved in how lucky we were. We could never have handled all these responsibilities of ranch life on our own, even if we were game to learn. But at Thomas Creek Ranch, we found ourselves with ten other families who knew what they were doing and were happy to share their knowledge and their wisdom. To some extent, it's a self-selecting community. No one would move in if they didn't want to cooperate.

CHAPTER 14

Surviving the Tailspin: Sticking to the Kindness Formula

Business at Ellie Mae was humming right along. We had hundreds of employees, and—as I reached maturity in my role as CEO and leader—it was important to me that my commitment to kindness was evident in the workplace. **Consultants would caution that I was overspending on expenses like our employees' medical insurance, but I wanted these folks to be cared for the way I would look after my own kids.** Even if it meant that I was footing the bill. It was selfish, really, in that I wanted our employees to be excited about coming to work. I wanted them to think: *Thank god it's Monday.*

My goal was to create a company culture where people felt valued and inspired, a place that felt good to be in every day. I knew that meant creating a fantastic work environment, so I focused on the details—little things that made my own life better. I would stop at Safeway on my way into the office and buy bunches of daffodils to put on people's workstations and on the reception desk. I filled the walls with art—first with posters, then giclee, and finally, when the company could afford it, we began acquiring original works. Over the years, we gathered enough of a collection to bring in an art curator to give tours and hold artist receptions. Company picnics and parties added dimension to the experience.

And it worked: Ellie Mae had close to zero employee turnover. In Silicon Valley, where everybody is poaching everybody else's employees, this was almost unheard of. But we genuinely wanted our employees to feel at home. In fact, in the first employee manual, the primary guideline was simply: "Don't do anything that would embarrass your mother." If an employee or their family member had medical expenses that weren't covered, we'd give them the money. And any employee with a child going to college had access to a $5,000 per year grant, per child. Ellie Mae was a family, and our employees felt that.

We went through a period with Ellie Mae where we knew the idea and the product were great, and knew we were ahead of the curve— but also knew we might be too far ahead. **For a startup to work, an idea needs to be ahead of its time, but not too far ahead—and the execution has to be, if not flawless, then effective and energetic, able to overcome setbacks and mistakes.** That was a point I made during my speech at the December 2000 Mortgage EC Conference on technology in the mortgage industry. "Consumers are just not ready to put their mortgage where their mouse is. That's the bad news. The good news is potential home-buyers are using the Internet to shop for loans and to compare rates. Consumers are demanding more information, and studies show that there is a shift underway."

In that speech I also shared the results of a study that Fannie Mae had conducted, which found that only 4 percent of respondents had at that point applied online for a mortgage, and half that number had completed the whole process on the Internet. On the other hand, two-thirds of young people in the study (eighteen- to twenty-four-year-olds) believed that most mortgages would be made online within five years. The tea leaves were not hard to read: Ours was a growth business.

We would just have to get our house in order before economic headwinds kicked up too strong. I talked to *Chicago Tribune* columnist Lew Sichelman in September 2003 and warned of what was to come. As Lew explained that month in his article, "The refinancing market has already slowed considerably as a result of higher rates, leaving lenders to battle over a much smaller mortgage pie. The resulting shakeout could be a bloodbath, warns Sig Anderman of Ellie Mae."

Bloodbath? That's not a word I would use. But the writer of the article did quote me directly saying: "It's going to be a painful next twelve months. There is only so much market share to go around."

I knew trouble was ahead, but—like everyone else—did not know for sure when it was coming. At Ellie Mae, we tried to focus on continuing to innovate and look ahead. Our mission was to automate anything that was automatable in the mortgage origination process—and that was everything! Just point and click to retrieve all the data and documents needed to fund a mortgage, like credit and title reports, appraisals, borrowers' income, and asset information. Everything.

As part of our loan automation systems, also in late 2003, we introduced a new program that focused on minority mortgage brokers and their clients, giving them detailed information on offerings specifically available to them as minority borrowers. For example, we wanted to help families with different generations living together who were seeking to apply jointly for a mortgage. These borrowers had historically had a difficult time.

"There isn't even a place on the standard loan application form for such families to provide all their multi-generational members' names," I told *Inman News* in October 2003.

We were building momentum, and in October 2004, Ellie Mae made *Inc.* magazine's list of the 500 fastest growing private companies in America. "The companies that made this list have thrived despite continued stagnation in the economy, posting an average year-over-year sales growth of 265 percent," the magazine wrote. "*Inc.* 500 companies posted aggregate 2003 revenue of $12.6 billion, and 82 percent of them were profitable. And while the United States shed 410,000 jobs in 2003, *Inc.* 500 companies provided employment for more than 70,000 people."

We were growing fast because we had a new product that people wanted. Our yearly revenue went from zero to a million to $3 million to $6 million—all the way up to $35 million in 2006 and $38 million in 2007. You could follow that line right on up, watching revenue continue to grow.

Then came 2008.

We'd branched out creatively. One step we'd taken was to link small mortgage brokers to bigger lenders like IndyMac, the Independent National Mortgage Corporation, based in Pasadena. In the early 2000s, half the mortgages written started with mortgage brokers. If there were ten million loans written in a year, five million were originated by mortgage brokers—and they could use our software to process mortgage loan applications and then connect to lenders to get their mortgages funded and earn a commission.

What exactly did mortgage brokers do? It was pretty simple. They found the borrower, handled the application, and put together all the information, data, and reports. Then they created an electronic loan package and sent that to a big lender. At that point it was: *Okay, fund this and pay us a $3,000 commission.*

By 2007, we had thousands of mortgage brokers on our network, linked to forty-five lenders funding loans for these small mortgage brokers. It was a good business with hundreds of credit reporting agencies, title companies, and appraisers. Brokers paid us a subscription fee for our software, as it helped them automate and streamline their mortgage processing, saving them time and money. And every time a broker ordered a credit report, an appraisal, a title report, or any other report the lender required, we'd get paid a small fee by the credit bureau, appraiser, title company, or whoever else got the business. And if they sent that file to the lender electronically, we integrated it into the lenders' processing systems, so they didn't have to duplicate any of the data and didn't have to retype anything—saving them time and money, and eliminating transcription errors. It was brilliant, great, no fuss, no bother. Hit click and send it off.

The program saved everybody time, money, headaches, errors, and embarrassment. When a broker sent a mortgage file to a lender over our network, we'd get twenty-five to forty dollars per loan, and it was click, boom, automatic. We never even sent out a bill. Everyone was billed automatically. If they didn't pay, you'd unplug them, and they knew it—so they paid. It was a great setup for us.

But the tougher economic climate was taking its toll, and in 2007 one of our lenders, New Century, ran into serious trouble. In February of that year, the Irvine-based company announced that it had made serious errors in accounting, reporting that it had actually lost $268 million in 2006. That April, New Century filed for Chapter 11 bankruptcy protection, sending shock waves throughout the industry. New Century was one of the big wholesale lenders funding loans for mortgage brokers using our software. As soon as I heard the news, I knew the outlook was grim. I called a meeting with Ellie Mae's management team.

"This is bad," I said. "No, it's worse than bad. It's huge. If they went under, others are going to go under, too. We could see a cascade of defaults."

I was the oldest and most optimistic person in the company, and some were surprised to see me painting such a bleak picture. I was just getting started.

"We've got to get through this," I told the management team. "It could be a disaster."

I had lived through my companies running out of money before, and I was *not* going to go through that again.

"I want you to figure out—by Monday—how we can get by with our expenses reduced by one-third so we know we can make it through this."

There were gasps in the room.

"I can't do it!" some told me.

"Word will get out that we're going out of business," someone else said. I waited for them to air out their concerns.

"Look," I answered, "I'd rather word go out that we're *going* out of business than word go out that we *went* out of business."

I let that sink in.

Setbacks and challenges are a given. You know they're going to come up; what matters is how you respond. All businesses have challenges, and software businesses have more, especially when you're on the leading edge—or, as I like to say, the bleeding edge—as we were in the early 2000s, establishing software as a service (SaaS).

We went through some major growing pains at Ellie Mae, but we had credibility because we always went out of our way to be kind, honest, above-board, and candid with our employees and customers. Earlier that year, I'd been planning another round of hiring to add 100 more jobs, bringing our total staff to 250. Instead, we had to make painful choices to whittle down to a work force of 164 employees.

"We've *got* to do this," I said, before breaking up the meeting.

I told everyone to enjoy their weekend, and I meant it. Maintaining optimism and compassion throughout such a difficult process was important to me because using kindness as a business strategy has another major advantage that might not be obvious to people: It can help you get through challenges.

When Monday came, several of the senior managers did not seem any more ready to do what I'd asked.

"Sig, you're not cutting out fat, you're cutting into muscle," one of them said, speaking for all of them.

I listened and I smiled. I was going to be as compassionate about this as I could. This was not about trimming muscle or fat, and it was not about whether nearly 100 of our employees deserved to be let go. This was about preparing for a major storm—or risk being swamped and capsizing. I knew that most new companies failed because they either grew too fast and outgrew their internal systems and controls, or they ran out of money. We were growing at a good pace and had our systems working well. I was determined that we would not run out of money—we had plenty in the bank, but if the economy continued to shrink, I was sure we would not be able to get more. The worst time to get investments is when you need them, and the prospect for the overall economy is gloomy.

"Guys, trust me, I don't like this any more than you do. But if we get through this, at least we'll have some money, and we'll be able to resume our growth," I said. "You have to do this, but I want you to do it in an intelligent and kind way. Reduce our workforce, so we can get by."

Here I turned to Lisa Bruun, our head of human resources, who was in the meeting. Lisa had been with me since almost the first year we were in business. She was sharp, dedicated to our company, and tough as nails. Everyone knew it and respected her.

Although I tried to maintain my kind tone, I needed them to know I was serious about this task. I didn't want to let people go any more than they did, and I wouldn't be asking this of them if we weren't in such dire circumstances.

"Look," I said. "If you can't do it, then Lisa will give me a list of all our employees, and I'm going to cross out every third name." I paused for a moment before continuing. "I'll do it. I will. I'll have to. I'd rather not. I would rather each of you do it in a way that's intelligent and informed."

It was then they saw I was dead serious.

This time I'd broken through. A couple days later, they came back and presented me with their plans for cutting staff. It was not pretty, but it was not brutal. We were as kind about it as we could be, explaining that our budgetary hand was forced. We gave each person a solid package of severance pay, allowed them to exercise their stock options, and committed to maintaining their medical insurance until their next job. We were happy to help them find new employment any way we could.

I was right about the coming storm. Within the year, forty-three of our forty-five lenders went out of business, and our brokers had no place to sell loans. It had all started with New Century, as I had warned. "The collapse of New Century ushered in a series of failures among mortgage lenders, ultimately rocking global financial markets, forcing banks around the world to write down or take losses on nearly $250 billion in mortgage-linked securities, and sending the U.S. housing market into a tailspin," *The New York Times* reported in April 2008.

Brokers, it turned out, took it on the chin for the financial collapse; they were accused of making bad loans that were poorly written. "As homeowners, shareholders and federal investigators pick through the subprime wreckage, many have asked how effectively front-line financial monitors carried out their duties," that same *Times* article concluded. "Ratings agencies responsible for signing off on the creditworthiness of securities, and regulators responsible for overseeing banking practices and safeguarding the entire financial system, have already been roundly criticized for not sounding alarms earlier."

We had survived the tailspin by reacting quickly to the shifting environment and making the difficult choices required to cut staff and give ourselves some maneuvering room. And while the survival needs of the company had to come first, none of us made decisions without compassion at the fore.

CHAPTER 15

Transparency and Productivity at Ellie Mae

Once we got through the worst days of 2007, it soon seemed that things were already getting better.

"I'm amazed we're doing as well as we are," I told *The New York Times* in January 2008. "We have a lot of irons in the fire. I think in the kind of turmoil we're experiencing, there is always opportunity."

That *Times* article, headlined "SOME ENTREPRENEURS PROSPER DURING U.S. HOUSING SLUMP," went on to lay out an optimistic vision of Ellie Mae's "bright future," even if not quite at the triple-digit rate of growth we'd hit at the outset, noting that "185,000 employees at 16,000 mortgage firms and banks" used our software.

"Last year, Ellie Mae reaped lavish returns on a product called Encompass Anywhere, a Web-based version of its software that is attractive to bigger brokerage firms because it is accessible from any computer and the firms do not have to maintain it," the *Times* continued. "Though the cost is $60 a month per 'seat' instead of $60 a year for use of the software not maintained by Ellie Mae, Encompass Anywhere has doubled the number of users to 16,000 [companies] since April 2005."

I wasn't trumpeting our success, but I was optimistic that events were going in our direction, and I predicted a rebound of business in late 2009. "Mortgage brokers who are still around then will survive," I told the *Times*. "The buzzwords right now are 'more scrutiny' and 'more efficiency.' That is music to our ears because that is what we provide."

In hindsight, I was lucky in another way, because Ellie Mae ended up with a dream team with combined capabilities far greater than any one person, including me, could ever have. This team power carried us through incredibly challenging times. Being caring and generous was my way of getting what was eventually a team of over 2,000 people to share my vision and make it come to fruition.

I always had a knack for dreaming big dreams, and envisioning new technologies and transformative ways of doing things. And, with my passion, I was able to motivate others to share my dreams—my wife, my family, employees, and investors. But that was pretty much where my skills ended. I needed people to execute and make those dreams a reality, and I was always motivated to nurture executive talent at Ellie Mae. I needed those talents—in engineering, in product development, in sales, in finance—because I had no experience in those areas. And no particular ability, frankly.

After fifty years in and around business, I'm convinced that it's very hard, if not impossible, to find all "A" players who are good at everything that needs to be done. **What you need is an A-Team. If you get enough smart, talented players with good synergy, and get them to work together, like and respect each other, and share a common vision, you end up with an A-Team.** I was candid with our leadership team that I needed them as much as they needed me. I could be the cheerleader and visionary. I could get people to fall in love with the company as investors or partners. **But I needed each**

of them to become a leader in their area of responsibility: technol-ogy, engineering, finance, sales, productive development.

I also tried hard not to breathe down their necks too much. **That's one of the knocks on entrepreneurs, that they can never keep their fingers out of everybody else's pie. Sure, I was tempted at times to put in more than my two cents, but over the years, I learned to hold my tongue and just let these people do what they know how to do.** It took me a long time to learn that lesson, but luckily I got there with Ellie Mae.

We ended up with a great leadership team, an A-Team that took us to what's known as a unicorn, a startup tech company that reached a billion-dollar valuation. We eventually reached "deca-corn" sta-tus, meaning we were worth at least $10 billion. The managers I nurtured became very successful and ultimately very well-rewarded financially. But we didn't always hire the right people. I don't know if it's even possible to *always* hire the right people. I learned from working with the recruiting professionals that even when you com-pletely vet a potential executive using a professional recruiter, run a thorough background check, and go through all the steps to do your due diligence, 40 percent of the time you will end up with the wrong hire. You're lucky if you bat .600; that's a better batting average than any baseball player can achieve over a season, but it makes disap-pointment an in-built part of the hiring process.

At Ellie Mae we had our share of wrong hires. Perhaps most painfully, we had to try multiple people as head of sales before we found Cathleen Schreiner Gates, a really talented woman who was a perfect fit. We hired Cathleen as senior vice president of sales and client services in March 2012 and she already had an impressive body of work behind her. In her ten years at Hyperion Solutions, a software company that Oracle acquired in 2017, she helped the com-pany grow its revenues from $10 million to $500 million. Cathleen was just phenomenal, and we were lucky to have her.

We had great stability with our Chief Technology Officer, Limin Hu, who co-founded Ellie Mae with me and served as our brilliant and capable CTO—and trusted partner—for a full twenty years, before shifting to CTO Emeritus in 2017.

And Jonathan Corr, who I hired in 2003, was another superstar performer. I hired Jonathan as a product manager to design Encompass, our mortgage broker and lender software. Jonathan had an engineering degree from Columbia and a Stanford MBA. He had previously worked for a paper mill company, and then Netscape, the first Internet browser, and then PeopleSoft, one of the first software companies automating business processes. It was the perfect background for Ellie Mae: knowledge and experience in engineering, business process automation, and user-friendly interfaces. And he knew nothing about mortgages. I loved that. He wasn't skeptical about a forty-five minute mortgage! Jonathan was brilliant, hard-working, and loyal, and fifteen years later, I chose him to succeed me as CEO.

With the position of Chief Financial Officer it was just the opposite. We went through three CFOs before Edgar Luce took over in July 2005. He started with us as a temp after we'd had to fire his predecessor, and might have seemed like the least likely to succeed—but he quickly flourished and grew in the role, making himself invaluable.

One of my early hires was Joe Tyrrell, a phenomenal person, team builder, and leader. Joe joined us from a local bank, where he had started in loan underwriting and, when we hired him, was in charge of their credit card division. At Ellie Mae for twenty years, Joe did everything, and eventually became President, succeeding Jonathan Corr. Joe is smart, innovative, and hard-working, with a wonderful sense of humor—and like every top leader in our company, a genuinely honest and caring person.

Our systems weren't that reliable at first—no one offering a SaaS (software as a service) solution had much luck. The engineering was tricky, with tens of thousands of users on different Internet networks and individual computers all linking into the same database housed on massive servers. We were too far ahead of the curve and suffered for it. Talking to frustrated customers whose systems weren't working for a few hours, with hundreds of employees sitting around idly, was particularly painful after my team and I had persuaded them to rely on us. "Use our system, not your local system," we'd tell clients. "We're more reliable." But it turned out we weren't.

Once again, being honest and committed to working with integrity got us through those challenges. We were upfront about problems that arose. We wouldn't try to point fingers at somebody else. We accepted responsibility when it was ours—and no matter whose problem it was, we would try to solve it. And we always did.

Over time, I also learned that sometimes what feels like being kind actually isn't. When I started out in business, I never wanted to tell employees about anything that was negative. I always felt like I had to be the cheerleader and protect them from bad news. Especially with a small company, I felt like we should never share the financials internally. Either way, it seemed to me, you would run into potential trouble. If the numbers were bad, I was afraid our employees would quit. And if the financial results were good, then they would ask me for a raise!

But guess what? It was actually a good thing to treat people as adults. I eventually matured into understanding that. By my Ellie Mae years, I was able to see and accept that the people I worked with weren't just employees, they were people who relied on me and this company for their livelihood and for their careers. They needed and wanted whatever information I could give them. **I learned that when we were running into trouble, the respectful, trusting approach was to share what's going on and make our employees part of the process and the solution rather than keeping them in the dark.** They're better off, and you're better off. It's kind—and it's also smart.

Once a month at Ellie Mae, we gathered everyone together for a general meeting. Mostly these gatherings were a lot of fun. I usually had some good news to impart, along with whatever else there was to bring up. Good or bad, surprising or unsurprising, I would go over it all in detail with everyone: here are our short and long term goals, here's where our financials are, here's how much money we have, here's what else we have to focus on moving forward. We're going to have to raise some more money because on this trajectory we are not going to be able to continue without another infusion of money. Here are the customers we want. Here are the challenges we face with the product. Here are the delays we are facing.

It wasn't just me up there talking, this was participatory. The head of the technology department would give a presentation, and then we would talk it over. Then the head of the engineering department gave us more to think about and if people had ideas to kick around, we kicked them around before moving on.

I adopted the open approach—call it nice as company policy—because it felt right. I didn't know if it would be a net plus or a net negative, in terms of how things worked out, I just knew that was how I wanted Ellie Mae to function. But it worked in spades. Trusting people to see the bigger picture paid off. Not only were they less spooked by hard times, but they also rallied behind the challenges we faced and pushed harder to figure out how we could solve a particular problem. How could we get a product to market faster? Who should we focus on to get these deals closed?

Through trial and error, we developed a corporate DNA that worked to our advantage and contributed to the company's success. A big part of this success was showing genuine kindness.

CHAPTER 16

Going Public

Everyone had blamed the mortgage brokers for the crisis we'd been through. Brokers were hammered in the press as the culprits, and within the industry they might have been taking even more heat—all of which was misplaced. Blaming brokers for what happened was like blaming an auto dealer for a lousy Ford truck you bought. It wasn't their fault; they were selling a truck that Ford manufactured. Brokers were only offering the loans with the borrower qualifications that Fannie Mae and the big banks had designed and were willing to buy.

After the 2008 meltdown, I'd been petrified that all our customers were going out of business and our revenue was dropping—though we were hanging on, still profitable, and we never, throughout all the turmoil, became unprofitable. To give you an idea of my mindset, the situation seemed so dire that I settled on the notion that we'd have to create our own big bank to fund these loans. It wasn't a bad idea. So I made a concerted effort to create a new mortgage bank, but couldn't quite pull that one off. And, as it turned out, thank goodness for that!

Meanwhile, the ground in the mortgage industry was shifting under our feet—in a good way. Business was picking up, thanks to a move we'd made a few years earlier away from mortgage brokers and toward smaller mortgage bankers. Originally, when we built the Ellie Mae software, it was intended for mortgage brokers who package the loan and give it to a lender; then the lender funds it and pays a commission. By 2005, we made a strategic decision to focus more on the small mortgage bankers, who actually wrote a check to fund the loan and then turned around and sold the mortgage to a bigger bank (Fannie Mae, Freddie Mac, or the Federal Housing Authority (FHA)), and made a profit on the sale. Just as we eventually did at my prior company, CompuFund.

We liked focusing more on the small mortgage bankers because brokers were not the ideal customers. There was very high turnover in the broker community. Basically, just about anybody could become a broker very quickly. It was easy in and easy out, so brokers didn't need or want as much firepower in their software, and therefore weren't willing to spend much money on it. One of our main competitors, Calyx, was selling brokers a perpetual license to its software for less than nine hundred bucks. For a forever license! You can't make money doing that because you have to keep updating the software and providing customer support. And their software didn't work well for mortgage bankers, who needed much more functionality.

So we targeted mortgage bankers. That's a category that also includes the big banks, like Chase and Wells Fargo, which all have mortgage banking operations. Many of our competitors—and we had a lot of them—were focusing on either small mortgage brokers or on the very big guys because of the large potential payout.

If you sell to Wells Fargo, they might pay you $30 million for a piece of software. Sounds great, right? Who wouldn't get a little starry-eyed thinking of banking thirty mil? The downside: To score that prize you probably needed at least five years to develop that complex, demanding software, which is hard, and you might or might not land the client. In fact, almost all of the competitors who took on this challenge broke their picks and went out of business. It was too much for them, trying to deal with the big banks, which all drove a hard bargain. They were big and not shy about throwing their weight around.

So we decided to turn our efforts toward the middle of the industry—not brokers, but also not very large banks and mortgage bankers. After speaking to dozens of customers and hundreds of their employees, we built and tested a comprehensive software package designed specifically for mortgage banks with somewhere between a few and a couple hundred employees. Coming out of the financial crisis of 2008, these smaller mortgage banks started doing very well. If the brokers were the bad guys, the smaller mortgage banks were somehow seen as the good guys. These small banks were flourishing, getting bigger and better, which meant that our businesses started picking up again. All the competitors were focused on building this very sophisticated software for massive banks and we had software that only fit the small to mid-sized bank; it was usable straight "out of the box," and could be easily configured to their specific needs.

We also came up with a canny concept called "success-based pricing"—credit for the idea goes to my eventual successor as CEO of Ellie Mae, Jonathan Corr. The idea was that customers only paid when they closed a loan. If they didn't close on any loans, they didn't have to pay us. If they did, we got $100 for each loan that closed. Since these smaller mortgage banks had just fought their way through the traumatic experience of a financial crisis where the mortgage industry basically stopped dead in its tracks, they were still a little shell-shocked. Our proposal was very appealing to them. Offering them this deal was also kind, a mutual benefit for both of us.

"Look, we're your partners," we'd tell these customers. "When times are good, you're going to pay us more, but you're going to be making a lot more. When times are bad, you're not going to pay us." They loved it.

Business ratcheted up so well from 2010 on that I decided in 2011 it was time to take the company public. For one thing, I turned seventy that year. I'd gone through the nightmare of being flat broke twelve years earlier when I was fifty-eight, having to go visit a bankruptcy attorney with Susan and question the entire foundation of my livelihood. We'd come through that dark period, and I'd built a good company in Ellie Mae, but I didn't have much to show for it. All of my net worth was in Ellie Mae stock, literally 100 percent. I was ready to start cashing out some of my stock and have some financial breathing room.

The venture capital (VC) system was set up to motivate you to take a company public if it had the goods to deliver. It had to do with the ownership structure when you raised startup funds from venture capitalists, who are investing to make a good return on their investment. They expect very high returns, because they are taking a very high risk. So they received what was called preferred stock for their investment. That meant if the company was sold privately, without going public, they got paid first. The stock everyone else bought was common stock, with no front-of-the-line privileges. Then, on top of that, the venture capitalists received their percentage share of whatever was left. But going public meant the preferences would be gone.

By 2011, investors had put about $85 million into Ellie Mae and owned half the stock. So if we sold the company privately, say for $100 million, the first $85 million would go to them to re-pay their investment, leaving $15 million to be divided up among all stockholders, including the investors. In that scenario, investors would get their $85 million back off the top, then get half of the $15 million that was left over—or a total of $92.5 million. I'd end up with one or two million after fifteen years of work building this company.

But if we went public, it would eradicate the special status of the VC's stock and they would become common stockholders. So if you sold the company for $100 million, the investors would get $50 million, leaving a bigger piece of the pie for the rest of us to divide. I'd end up with $10 million—a much better result for me. The other employees would also end up with a better slice.

Beyond that, assuming the company was not sold after we went public—and we had no intention of selling it—all the stockholders, including me, would have the ability to sell shares of their stock from time to time on the open, public stock exchange, and have liquidity. And if the company did well, the stock price would go up over time. The other shareholders and I loved the idea of being able to sell shares of stock little by little, generate cash, and still retain ownership. It would be a terrific outcome after years and years of hard work by everyone.

Once we made the decision to go public, it was exciting. I had a friend at Goldman Sachs, and he offered to have the institution take us public. The board's reaction was unanimous: "You can't go wrong with Goldman Sachs." It was a feather in our cap, as a small company, to have Goldman behind us.

But my attorney was not as excited as I was.

"Sig, get two underwriters to do it jointly," he urged me. "That way, if one of them decides to pull out at the last minute, you've got a back-up."

It made sense. You could use Goldman, but also Morgan Stanley, J.P. Morgan, or one of the others as a co-underwriter in the offering. I got my friend at Goldman on the phone and told him what my attorney was advising.

"Listen, if you want to have a second underwriter, we don't want to do the deal," he said. "Sig, you don't need a second underwriter. We won't pull out. We'd never screw you. We're friends."

Raise your hand if you see where this is going—a new definition of "never!"

I stuck with Goldman Sachs, and we went through the process of writing the prospectus for the road show. It was a crazy process that took us a year, and it cost $2.5 million—most of that in legal fees.

Three or four weeks before we were ready to do the roadshow, Goldman Sachs called and asked for a meeting. What could possibly be up? These friends who had looked me in the eye and said they would never, ever screw me now proceeded to tell me that yes, they were screwing me.

"Sig, we can't do this," they told me. "There's not enough interest. The mortgage industry is still shaky from the financial crisis. Fannie Mae is still in receivership. We can't do the deal. We're pulling out."

I was flabbergasted.

"*What?*" I said. "You told me you'd never pull out."

We were suddenly dead in the water. I'd shelled out $2.5 million to get this prospectus done, and we had nothing we could do with it.

Luckily, our attorney introduced us to Barclays, a big stock underwriter based in London, and they agreed to do the deal. It was back on: We would get the roadshow going with a week in Europe, starting in London. It would be Jonathan, me, and Ed Luce, our Chief Financial Officer. We'd see what kind of reception we got in Europe. It would be a trial balloon for the climate worldwide.

As the date for the roadshow kick-off approached, the excitement—and pressure—built. Barclays kept sending all of us emails reminding us to make sure we each had a valid passport with six months remaining. Did they think I'd never been on a plane before?

The morning of the flight, however, I was in a panic. Sure enough, I could not find my passport. I was looking all over the house. I just had it! I just saw it!

"Susan, where's my passport?" I asked my wife.

She had no idea. She joined in the search, along with our daughter, Elissa. We combed through the whole house and couldn't find my passport anywhere, so I drove into the office. Had I somehow left it there? Apparently not.

I was unbelievably embarrassed. They had been telling me for weeks to check my passport and my reaction was: *Of course. What moron wouldn't have his passport?* That moron, apparently, would be me! And while I was searching, the plane to London—with Jonathan, Ed, and all the underwriters on board—took off without me.

Elissa managed to find a place in San Francisco where you could get a passport the same day, one of only a few places in the entire United States that would do it that fast. I had to call our team and tell them I would do my best to get to London one day later.

I made it eventually, and the road show went off like gangbusters. They loved us everywhere we went: London, Frankfurt, Paris, Milan. We were a good team: I could tell the story of Ellie Mae and how we automated things, saying you didn't have to have an MBA to conclude that getting a mortgage ought to be automated. Jonathan would jump in to talk about the details of the technology and Ed would handle the financials. It was a great roadshow. We were a roaring success in Europe.

For the U.S. roadshow, the underwriter gave us a private jet, a G5, for a week, so we could fly from city to city, explaining Ellie Mae and its potential as a public company to dozens and dozens of potential institutional investors. It looked pretty good, but not like it had in Europe. U.S. investors, led by the pension funds and the likes of T. Rowe Price, Fidelity, and Franklin Templeton, were all still spooked by the recent history of the mortgage industry. They were still smarting from its major collapse just three years earlier.

The underwriter told us we looked okay. We were generating interest. We were hopeful we'd hit our target and go public at $12 a share for a valuation of $280 million. By the last couple of days, I suggested Susan join us in the G5 and bring our grandson Simon. There was plenty of room. They could fly around with us. It was a skate to the finish line, and it would be poignant to have Susan and Simon there with me. And a real kick to be riding on a private jet!

We were in Chicago the last night before the stock was supposed to be allocated. We had another of those typical days on the road where we started meetings at 6:30 a.m. and went straight through with no breaks until 7 p.m. As I ran out of steam, I got tired of hearing the sound of my own voice, and would sometimes lose all sense of what I was saying. That night, they called me into a meeting room at the private jet terminal.

"Sig, we can't close the deal," they told me. "We don't have enough support for it. The stock will crater. You should put it off for a year."

I was crestfallen.

"Everybody is still too spooked by the financial crisis," they continued. "Ellie Mae is a high tech company providing software and systems for the mortgage industry. The investors who typically invest in high tech stocks don't understand the mortgage business and are afraid of it, and the mortgage investors don't understand the high tech business and are intimidated by it. We can't do it."

I wasn't giving up that easily. I didn't believe our goose was really cooked.

"Well, there has to be a price where you'd get enough buyers," I said. "If it doesn't sell at twelve, then maybe we do it at ten, or eight, or two. Tell me, what would the price be that would be low enough to be able to close tomorrow?"

They huddled and came back and told me: $6. That did not sound so terrible to me. I was not interested in selling my stock right away anyway. So there was time for the stock price to come up, the way I saw it. If the company performed the way I was sure it would, the stock price would come around. I asked if it mattered whether the stock started at $6 and worked its way up to $30 within a couple years, or started higher and still got to the same price. No, the answer came. It didn't matter.

It sounded workable. We did not need the cash for the company. There wasn't a debt or loan that needed repaying. I just wanted to go public to create liquidity for myself and for the other shareholders— and to get rid of the preference of the investors. So I quickly called a board meeting together.

"Don't go public at $6," just about all of them told me. "It's an embarrassment. It will be a penny stock."

"Look," I said. "I'm seventy years old. If we wait a year, who knows? The market could crash again and then we would have to wait another two or three years. Then I'm seventy-five and we could hiccup as a company."

I felt I was winning them over.

"No, you can't do it, because then you can't get listed on the New York Stock Exchange," the attorney said. "Your total company value has to be more than $150 million, and you'd only be at $140."

We'd have to go onto the American Stock Exchange, which is a division of the New York Stock Exchange, with much less appeal than the NYSE. That didn't faze me, either. So we'd wait until our value was more than $150 million and then make the move to the New York Stock Exchange. Finally, I had everybody convinced.

"Listen, we've got to do it now," I said. "If it's $6, we'll make it happen. In three years, it will be $20 or $30 anyway."

We went public, and for a year the stock stayed where it was, and even dropped down below $4 for a while. But after a year it came up enough that we could move to the New York Stock Exchange. Quarter by quarter, we kept posting strong earnings reports, but the stock stayed low. Too many investors were still worried about another mortgage crisis.

Thankfully, by 2014, we were rolling. Investors and Wall Street analysts were becoming believers. By that October, our stock price had climbed to $38, a 44 percent increase for the year. That month, Bloomberg published an article about our strong growth that started off: "Ellie Mae Inc., a technology firm that processes almost a quarter of U.S. mortgage applications, is growing so quickly it ran out of room at its San Francisco Bay Area headquarters and had to cram software engineers into its gym."

That was true. For the year, we had the best performing stock on the New York Stock Exchange. Once we hit $30, that gave us a valuation of $1 billion, making us a unicorn. Back then that made us a rarity. Before long, the stock would hit $100 a share.

CHAPTER 17

Sig's Bees

Even as I was celebrating our victories with Ellie Mae, I was finding other sources of sweetness in life. One of my favorite byproducts of living at Thomas Creek Ranch was my new hobby—beekeeping. That too came about by sheer good luck. One Saturday morning, Susan and I looked out the kitchen window and saw a massive swarm of bees, flying so tightly together we could barely see daylight through them. But within an hour or so they had all flown into a small box outside our front door and disappeared. If we hadn't watched what was happening, we wouldn't have known they were there.

I decided to call a local beekeeper, who came the next day and helped me transfer the bees to a Langstroth hive—one of those white boxes you sometimes see lining fields in the countryside. And that was the beginning of my beekeeping hobby. I took courses at the local junior college, read every book I could find, and watched endless YouTube videos. Over the next decade, I ended up producing more honey than my family and friends and I could consume. So I began giving it to employees and customers of Ellie Mae. The demand for honey grew to the point that I was producing 3,000 jars of honey a year, from my own four hives and several dozen set up for me by a friendly local beekeeper.

To this day, you can find my beekeeping website, "Welcome to Sig's Bees," online at www.sigsbees.com. There's artwork of the bucolic scene at Thomas Creek Ranch, with the fence, chickens, and the sun shining down on a large tree. Next to a picture of me, smiling, visitors to the site can read a welcome note: "Beekeeping is a fascinating way to experience the natural process of making honey. Ever wondered where that jar of honey comes from?" I'm not sure the beekeeping video we posted still works; might depend on your computer.

Life in Forestville brought me full circle. It was the ranch I'd envisioned since I was a boy growing up in New York City. When I moved to California to run various businesses, I put my years as an environmental lawyer behind me, but in Forestville, I also found myself in a familiar role, advocating.

In March 2003, I wrote a Letter to the Editor published in the *Sonoma West Times and News*, which read as follows:

> On behalf of the Forestville Planning Association, I would like to urge a denial of the application of Forestville LLC requesting a Federal Clean Water Act Section 401 Certification for the Empire Self Storage Project. We believe it is inappropriate, if not presumptive, for the applicant to propose destroying a natural wetland area (hundreds if not thousands of years in the making) and, in its place, attempting to 'build' an artificial wetland, requiring monitoring, reviews, mitigations, and periodic assessments by regulatory agencies. (What if they don't comply with the conditions imposed? Or what if the 'built wetland' doesn't do what it is supposed to?) Our wetlands are an essential part

of our ecosystem. They are endangered, few and far between, and, once destroyed, are gone. ... We submit that the role of the North Coast Regional Water Quality Control Board is to protect our water sources, not acquiesce in their destruction. There is no compelling need for storage units on this site that would justify sacrificing this natural resource.

It was a heck of a letter! Not exactly arguing before the Supreme Court with David Sive, but in some ways writing and publishing it felt just as good. There were many environmental fights to take on, from advocating for the wetlands to blocking the expansion of local quarries. This last fight led to putting limits on quarry expansion in Forestville, and a colorful lead paragraph in the *Sonoma West Times and News*: "A local citizen's group recently won a lawsuit that will be paid off in cold, hard rock," reporter David Abbott wrote. "The California Superior Court has awarded $155,000 to Forestville Citizens for Sensible Growth to reimburse the group for legal fees incurred in its multi-year lawsuit opposing the expansion of Canyon Rock Quarry on the north side of Forestville."

"We are gratified the Court recognized our pivotal role in protecting the rights of all citizens to participate in decisions affecting our fragile environment," I said on behalf of the group in a statement at the time. "The award of attorney's fees is a way to at least partially level the playing field."

It was a meaningful victory—for us, and for the cause.

CHAPTER 18

Stepping Down as CEO

The time came when I knew I had to consider stepping down as CEO of Ellie Mae. I was seventy-five years old. What if I keeled over one day? What if I was in intensive care, incapacitated, and nobody was there to take over the day-to-day leadership of the company? I couldn't let that happen. It would not be fair to our employees or our investors, and it would also not be fair to my family, since our entire net worth was in Ellie Mae stock.

I also knew I wanted the handover to be textbook. We had a remarkable run of handling challenges in just the right way at Ellie Mae, even when that seemed highly unlikely, and of using challenging transitions to break new ground. The word was that entrepreneurs might be well suited to start companies, but they were ill-equipped to actually *run* companies—I'd disproven that one, having started the company with Susan in our living room and running it for more than fifteen years.

The next rap was that an entrepreneur could never hand over the CEO position gracefully. I wanted to prove that one wrong as well, and did a lot of reading on the subject. I talked to a dozen CEOs who had successfully retired. And a few who hadn't. How do you make the move? What do you try to avoid? What are the important details of making it work smoothly?

One conclusion that I came to was that this could not be a gradual, ambiguous move. It had to be clear and decisive. This was not my immediate impulse. The truth was: I loved being CEO. I didn't want to go anywhere. I loved working with a lot of smart people, delegating to them, and helping them achieve great results. I didn't want to give that up, but I felt a strong sense of responsibility to prepare for a succession.

So at first, I tried to think in terms of a phased approach. Maybe there would be advantages to leaving gradually, greater ease for myself and the company? I took the idea to a close friend, Steve Vermut, a successful entrepreneur in his own right.

"No," he said, "don't phase out. Just do it now: Turn over the reins. If you try to make it gradual, everyone will continue to report to you."

"Really?" I said.

I'd let myself get used to the idea of a slow shift.

"Yes, for sure," my friend said. "You need to make a quick and decisive change in top leadership. That way, if your successor stumbles, you're still alive and vibrant. You can step in to help set things right."

Next up I had to sell the board on my decision—the company was on a roll, I was healthy, and the board felt that my chosen successor, Jonathan Corr, who was brilliant, but very brash, was not quite ready. Jonathan always had good ideas, and had risen from product management to CSO to COO in 2011, and then to president of Ellie Mae in 2013. To me, it was inevitable that Jonathan would take over as CEO, but this wasn't so evident to everyone else.

Jonathan rubbed some people the wrong way. In fact, a lot of people actively disliked him, and some even refused to work with him. He was extraordinarily competent, but he would often insult people in meetings, and was very difficult to collaborate with. This had to change. So I sent Jonathan to a two-week leadership development course, and hired an executive coach to build his kindness muscle and take the sharpness off some of his rough edges. He learned to be more compassionate with his colleagues, to listen more, yell less, and to let people flourish in their own right. It was a remarkable transformation.

We announced the coming changes months in advance—both to give people in the company time to get used to the idea of me no longer being CEO, and so as not to alarm Wall Street analysts, who are always spooked by unanticipated leadership changes. But even as the handover approached, I still had a hard time believing—or accepting—that it would really happen. It was very hard for me to imagine. And I worried about the consequences: My entire net worth was tied up in Ellie Mae, and if something happened with the company, my family would suffer.

Then in early 2015, we finally made the move. I became executive chairman and Jonathan took over as CEO. Far from cratering, the stock actually went up on the news! Okay, it only went up a point, but still. No ten-point drop! No panic that the great founder was retiring!

We put out a press release on January 5, 2015, announcing the change, effective February 1, which quoted me talking up Jonathan as an outstanding young business leader instrumental in the growth of the company—which he was—and had me saying I was "pleased to pass the baton"—which I sort of was.

"Sig had a vision when he founded the company seventeen years ago that Ellie Mae would fundamentally change the mortgage industry by automating everything possible in the origination process," Craig Davis, a longtime member of our board of directors, was quoted. "As one of the leading forces for change, Ellie Mae has helped transform the mortgage industry."

That we had, but if Ellie Mae was going to continue to make an impact, it would be without me in the top leadership. For three months, I didn't even set foot in the office. That way, I wouldn't be able to breathe down necks, look over shoulders, or second-guess Jonathan or anyone else.

Up to that point, Ellie Mae could have been a Harvard Business School case study. Every headache you could have, we had, but time and again we had tough calls to make and our choices turned out to be right. We had very few big stumbles and a lot of good choices that happened to work out well for us. In hindsight, we often made the right decisions even when taking another path would have been just as logical and defensible. We were lucky.

CHAPTER 19

An Initiative Clouded by Tragedy

One of our more satisfying innovations at Ellie Mae involved knocking down our walls—and I do mean literally. As the business grew, and as we hired more and more people, we did what a lot of companies had then, which was to give everyone their own cubicles. At one point, our new head of software development decided to get rid of the cubicles. He and the engineering team, which by then had grown to several hundred people, thought it was the thing to do—it was the latest Silicon Valley fad. Suddenly, instead of seeing nothing but plush gray cubicle walls everywhere, we could see each other. We could look into the faces of the many engineers and other technical people we'd added to the company.

So the walls came down, and I got to see everyone all at once. Surveying those faces, I had an immediate uncomfortable feeling, one of those "What's not right with this picture?" moments. There were hardly any Black or brown people.

"We need to hire more engineers of color," I told Lisa Bruun, our Vice President of Human Resources.

"We sure do," she said.

Her answer threw me.

"So why don't we?" I asked.

"Because they aren't out there," she explained.

The extreme shortage of qualified tech workers of color hit me as both utterly shocking, and as a human tragedy. Despite my initial shock, it wasn't surprising: I knew that, for generations, way too many in the Black community had been systemically thwarted, and stuck in the socioeconomic underclass. There was a lot of room for discussion about that stark reality—the legacies of slavery, denial of property to Black people and the generational impacts thereof, targeted incarceration, and institutional racism—but I wanted to focus on making at least a small difference in the arena of getting people good jobs that could lead to even better economic opportunity. There we were, the richest society in the history of the universe, and many people—through no fault of their own—were still born into circumstances that left them stuck in this low-flying orbit.

What made the situation even more tragic was that there were hundreds of jobs to be had, if there were candidates to fill them. We always had challenges with hiring people who had the basic qualifications we needed at Ellie Mae, and tech people in particular. In fact, during the first two decades of the twenty-first century, there was a constant shortage of tech talent in the United States. At one point, there were over one million tech job openings going unfilled.

The situation in Silicon Valley and its surroundings was even more dramatic. There were thousands of companies looking for talent. But competing against Facebook and Google and the other tech giants wasn't easy. We kept our employees once they were with us, but it was hard to compete with high-profile companies offering their employees perks like dog walkers, laundry service, car detailing, and gourmet cafeterias.

This was the picture that came together when we broke down the walls at Ellie Mae and looked out to see hundreds of people working on the floor. I could count the number of Black employees on one hand. I didn't like any of the answers I was getting when I complained about the situation, so I decided it was time to get creative, generate some fresh solutions, and start minting high-tech employees ourselves.

To me it seemed obvious. There were a million job openings across the country and not enough candidates to fill them. There were tens of thousands—if not hundreds of thousands—of unemployed or underemployed young people of color. Many would welcome a shot at an entry-level tech job that would open doors and—at least in some cases—position them to be the managers, executives, and even the entrepreneurs of tomorrow, maybe one day launching their own startups. They just needed enough training to fill the jobs and then perform.

We broke it down as an engineering problem. What, specifically, would it take to offer the training that would qualify people to take these jobs that were begging to be filled? Having retired as CEO, I had the time to figure it out. I spent a year talking to different people about what it would really take to make it happen—potential employers, colleges, junior colleges, tech schools—even an Army commander responsible for teaching computer programming. Do we have to take high school graduates and put them through college? Do we put them through a training course? What could work? What are the criteria that would need to be met to make someone qualified for a basic tech job like customer support or an entry-level position in cybersecurity, network operations, or even programming?

I reached out to my friend Landon Taylor, who I met twenty years previously when he was an executive at First American Title. Landon is an amazing guy, an inspiring leader who has served in a variety of executive roles in real estate and technology services. As a Black man in these industries, he had long taken an interest in diversifying engineering and computer-science talent. Landon shared his expertise and introduced me to many others who could share theirs, and help us to develop a curriculum.

We focused on the question of why there were so few Black people applying for even the most basic entry-level jobs We figured out that yes, we could take an average high-school graduate, a B or C student even, and in nine months give them the training to be fully qualified for one of those jobs. That might not sound like much, but for young people a job like that is a gateway. It opens up other possibilities. If you're diligent, reliable, and work hard, you've got great career potential. If you learn as you go, and keep mastering new skills, you can go wherever your heart takes you. Not everyone given that opportunity would put that much into it, it would depend on the individual. But in giving people options and opening doors for them, you gave them a shot at determining their own fate.

My wife Susan came up with a name for the program—the Springboard Initiative. I decided it was worth investing my own money in a pilot program, and ended up seeding $750,000. I knew if I focused on trying to line up funding from other sources, government or otherwise, the process would be endless, time-consuming, and demoralizing. We might never get anywhere. We would benefit more by self-funding and getting right to work. Then we would have the freedom to improvise along the way and make some real-time tweaks. If we were accountable to a board of directors, or funders, we'd face limitations on any adjustments in concept or implementation we wanted to pursue.

To run the program, I hired Sonya Brunswick, who had previously worked for two years as Executive Director of the Maisin Scholar Award Program in the Bay Area, and before that was Program Director for the San Francisco School Alliance. She also had a background in tech, as a network engineer, had served as a youth pastor in Japan, and spent three years in Germany as Director of Bitburg Protestant Youth of the Chapel.

After almost a year of research, planning, and developing the curriculum, we announced the program in June 2016 in local San Francisco Bay Area high schools, the YMCA, and youth organizations. We got over 100 applications in a matter of weeks, and chose fifteen recent high-school graduates. On a reasonable budget, we could educate, mentor, train, and support our pool of students. As Sonya said in a video about the program, "Our young people come from communities that are marginalized and undersold—my community."

Sonya handled day-to-day operations and worked directly with the young adults and with the training facilities where we held the program. Rather than building our courses from scratch, we realized it would be more efficient to send participants to local community colleges for as much of the curriculum as possible. We provided other tutorials, like how to prepare for a job interview, how to dress for work (even in casual California), and leadership training. Visa and Ellie Mae both agreed to sponsor the program as well—not as a favor to me, but because they thought it was a promising model—and we partnered with City College of San Francisco and the Bayview Hunters Point YMCA to provide the classroom space and teachers.

"You tend to grow more in a situation where you're not comfortable," one of the participants explained in our promotional video. "So when you step out of your box into a challenging situation, you always end up growing more."

We had in mind an ambitious goal of scaling up the project from that first test run and had people rooting for us. In October 2016, the *San Francisco Business Times* reported on our "lofty mission of placing 100,000 black young adults in STEM careers across the country within the next ten years" and added that we "just might be able to pull it off."

"There is a massive and insatiable demand for tech talent—and not just in Silicon Valley and San Francisco," I told the *Business Times*. "At the same time, there's a whole subsection of society that is talented and could fill these positions, but is under-resourced."

Flash forward a year: We pulled it off! Of the fifteen kids who went through the program that first year, thirteen of them made it through and immediately got jobs paying $50,000 a year. It didn't take any arm-twisting or sweet-talking of any companies for them to get those jobs; they were hired because there was a need, and they were well-qualified candidates. I knew if we could scale up the program, we could train many more people, maybe hundreds per year.

The graduation ceremony for the thirteen kids who made it through the program was a joyous occasion. Former San Francisco Mayor Willie Brown, once one of the most powerful politicians in the state, delivered a powerful and inspiring graduation speech as the master of ceremonies. Willie spoke from the heart, as someone who rose from poverty to become the highest elected Black official in the United States, prior to the election of Barack Obama as president. Here were 200 people—friends and families of the graduates—excited uncles and aunts, parents, siblings, and friends, all dressed to the nines. It was fabulous.

Eager to see the program grow even more, I turned to Gerald Chartavian, who I had met during my initial research for Springboard, to move the project forward. Gerald, a Harvard Business School grad, founded the hugely successful nonprofit Year Up to train underserved communities. He is a wonderful human being, brilliant and inspiring, and early on, I thought we might work together to explore different approaches to helping train young tech workers.

The reach of Year Up is amazing. Gerald grew up in a humble family in Lowell, Massachusetts, the son of a dentist and dental hygienist, and in 2014, he was celebrated with a segment on CBS News' *Sixty Minutes*, highlighting his work training and mentoring more than 2,000 young people a year from diverse backgrounds. That segment attracted more corporate sponsors and helped Gerald expand Year Up—and their work is still going strong all these years later.

The Springboard model was similar but distinct. Gerald's approach was to establish his own classroom facilities, hire his own teachers, and set it all up from scratch. I didn't think it made sense to build and maintain all that infrastructure, when community colleges were already there—and underutilized, to boot. So for Springboard, we decided to "subcontract" out the training to community colleges because they had the facilities and teachers already in place. It was a model I had come to understand during my years in business. **Don't always try to reinvent the wheel. If you don't need to build it yourself, and can buy or rent it, then do that.**

Gerald and I talked over the advantages and disadvantages of the two approaches, and over the years he shifted Year Up's operations to adopt the Springboard model of contracting out to community colleges. If we helped Gerald in his work, so much the better. Year Up is now training over 5,000 young underprivileged students a year, and is on track to hit 100,000 in ten years. One way or another, I feel we accomplished our goal. As Gerald once said, "The best thing we can do for a young person is to expect a lot from them."

Launching the Springboard Initiative was a very important part of my life. It was a challenge, taking on this glaring problem and working to arrive at fresh solutions that could be widely applied. Our work made a big difference in these kids' lives—and served as a model for Year Up and dozens of other organizations. We proved that we could transform people's lives within a year or less—and at relatively low cost. By the time we concluded our pilot and transferred the project to Year Up to continue, we knew that we could train someone in nine months for less than $30,000. What a great way to put kindness to work.

It should be no surprise that what young people of all backgrounds want, the world over, is a chance at a better life. A friend of mine visited Gaza recently for a tech conference, and even there, in a community of two million people largely isolated from the rest of the world, what young people wanted most were the tools to build their own companies—in short, their own futures.

As a public school teacher back in the Bronx more than fifty years earlier, I'd witnessed firsthand the power of helping young people onto a different life trajectory. I knew that even a small shift on one's path could translate into incalculable gains—and that's just what Year Up offers in communities nationwide.

Tragically, just a few months after Susan named the Springboard Initiative, she was diagnosed with pancreatic cancer. It all happened in a kind of blur. One day my beloved wife of fifty years was her usual healthy, vivacious self, full of life and enthusiasm for music and the arts and her family, and four months after the diagnosis, on January 7, 2017 she died in my arms. We were together with her, as a family, holding hands, surrounding her in love right up until she took her last breath.

I was very lucky to share fifty-two years with a woman who brought such joy to my life and opened up so much for me. And, in all honesty, I felt fortunate to be able to be with her and provide comfort as she died. It was painful and heartbreaking, of course, but at the same time it was a profoundly spiritual and moving experience. Susan and I grew up together, went through trauma and triumphs, and now we shared the most momentous—and tragic—of all life's experiences.

Over time, thoughts of Susan would go from mainly tears to mainly smiles, as recollections of the wonderful life we had together overcame the mourning. She was consummately kind to the very end, the source of my inspiration to innovate and find ever more compassionate ways to care for our family, and the world.

CHAPTER 20

Reflections on Business and the Sale of Ellie Mae

Another innovation we made at Ellie Mae was to be one of the early companies to embrace a model of software as a service—what came to be known as the SaaS sector. In the 1990s, that was unheard of. If you wanted new software, you went to the store and bought a CD, which made sense in a world of slow download speeds. That all changed with broadband.

We were one of the first companies to skip the disks and have our customers dial straight into our servers. If we had a client that was a company with 100 employees, then none of those employees had software from us on their machines, but they could all dial into our servers. This was a novel approach at the time, and for some clients it felt like a big leap.

"Do it this way," I'd tell the clients, looking them in the eye. "It's more reliable, and it's more secure. Trust me."

It was all that—I was good at selling our product because I genuinely believed in it myself. I really felt like all our customers—there were about 2,000—were more like friends than clients. I treated them as partners and didn't just like them, I *loved* them. That was genuinely how I felt. Call that the power of kindness, or just call it a lucky guy who after years of hard work got to do what he loved with people he loved.

One big difference between the East Coast, where I grew up, and the West Coast, where I made my new life, was in the distinction between work and personal relationships. It's just a generalization, not a hard and fast rule, but long before Silicon Valley companies were starting fashion trends with a relaxed, casual approach to clothing, people in California were more relaxed and casual with each other, more natural and direct. Think about it: If you can wear shorts and flip-flops at a business meeting instead of a tie (think Brad Pitt in *Moneyball*), it probably follows that you're going to feel more comfortable just being yourself and treating potential clients closer to the way you would treat friends, not as targets to be neutralized or conquered.

In some ways the word "businesslike" conveys useful concepts. From the time I was a young attorney in New York learning from the great environmental lawyer David Sive, to my first days in California, to my experiences with startups in the years since, one of my core values was always an insistence on high standards: hire good people and demand of them that they challenge themselves to do great work, day in and day out; consistently come up with fresh ideas; and maybe now and then deliver a bold and original insight. **You can be nice and still make clear that you're going to have very little patience for anyone phoning it in, cutting corners, or trying to fudge anything or mislead anyone. You can be demanding but also kind, serious but also seriously committed to having good relationships with everyone in the company.** This was the way I approached my role as CEO of Ellie Mae.

I was proud that everyone who worked for us had stock options. Top executives in the company obviously had more stock options than support staff or the guy who fixed the telephones in the office when something went wrong—but the point was, they all had stock options. They were all poised to benefit as the company went from fledgling startup to unicorn—and beyond. I figured: *If I go to the bank, let them all go to the bank with me.* And they did!

The value of the stock kept rising until about 2017 when the boom in SaaS companies like ours suddenly took a hit. On top of that, when the mortgage sector took a hit that same year, we missed our earnings target for the first time in eight years. Suddenly our stock was dropping. It sank from $105 a share to around $60 per share, and hung around $65.

For whatever reason, maybe because it was as obvious to others as it was to us that we were currently being undervalued, private equity investors started sniffing around. We became a target. I really didn't want to hear any of it, but we had fiduciary responsibilities as a board to entertain any reasonable offers. The next thing we knew, our attorneys were reporting back that an offer had been made to acquire Ellie Mae at $99 a share.

I did not want to sell. The offer sounded way too low to me. I thought we were worth double that, easily. I liked things the way they were. Jonathan was CEO and doing a great job. I could have my cake and eat it too, popping into the office as executive chairman whenever I wanted, giving a little advice, hugging people, and soaking it all in. Although the stock had dropped by a third, the business itself was booming, laying the groundwork for continuing growth and success. I'd go to conferences from time to time and talk about industry trends. It was all great fun for me. I would have loved to watch that play out with nothing changing at Ellie Mae—but as it turned out, my opinion on that count didn't matter all that much. My attorney laid that out for me in stark terms.

"Look," he said, "if you don't accept a $99 offer when the stock is at $65, you guys are going to get sued."

He stared at me and let that sink in.

"There's no wiggle room," he said. "It's a blatant conflict of interest. You're almost inviting a lawsuit at that point. If word gets out you turned down an offer so you could walk around at a convention, reveling in the success of your company, you really might get sued."

We agonized for a long time. I loved the company and hated the idea of selling, but in the end I just didn't feel there was a choice. It was time to pull the trigger and take the deal. So we sold the company for $3.7 billion to Thoma Bravo, a private equity firm that had the goal of holding the company for four or five years and then doubling its investment.

Here's how *The New York Times* reported on the deal in February 2019:

> No, this isn't about Fannie Mae. And don't get confused with Jed Clampett's hayseed daughter Elly May on *The Beverly Hillbillies*, either. It's Ellie Mae, the publicly traded provider of mortgage-processing software-as-a-service to American home lenders. The investment firm Thoma Bravo is paying $3.7 billion to acquire the Pleasanton, Calif.-based Ellie Mae. That's more than twenty-five times the software company's projected earnings before interest, taxes, depreciation and amortization for this year, according to estimates collated by Refinitiv, and a nearly 50 percent premium to its stock's latest thirty-day closing average. It's a pretty price to pay for exposure to a market that is being buffeted by rising interest rates, slipping home-price gains and worries about affordability. The Mortgage Bankers

> Association believes that United States home-loan originations declined by a little over 5 percent last year to $1.6 trillion. But such headwinds make the cost benefits of outsourced automation all the more attractive to lenders. … And investors seem to believe the sky is the limit for cloud-based software services. That may explain why Ellie Mae's stock traded slightly above the offer price for much of the day on Thursday, suggesting that Thoma Bravo's $99-a-share offer may not be the final word.

At that valuation, every share-holder received $99 per share when the deal closed on April 17, 2019, which meant that in one stroke we had created more than 100 millionaires who worked for us. Many of these were people who never dreamed of having that kind of money. I had people coming to me crying tears of joy. Some of them never had more than $5,000 in their banking account in their whole lives, and suddenly they checked their balances and saw seven figures. I loved it. We all did well in the deal. We had all worked passionately and hard, and we could all share in the rewards.

The company continued to prosper. The board members were all out, including me, once Thoma Bravo made the purchase, but Jonathan was still CEO and doing a great job. A little over a year later, another buyer came in—Intercontinental Exchange purchased Ellie Mae from Thoma Bravo for $11 billion in September 2020. Thoma Bravo had tripled their money in less than eighteen months—with a $7 billion profit. By then I was pretty much out of the picture, and the sale had little direct impact on me, but Jonathan and many others I'd worked with did very well in the deal. It was a dramatic end to a story that started when Susan and I first dreamed up Ellie Mae in our living room.

CHAPTER 21

The Maui Model

After Susan's death and my retirement from Ellie Mae, I realized I was ready for a change. My daughter Gabby had been living on the island of Maui, in Hawai'i, for a number of years, along with her husband, Bennett, and their children, Izzy and Sabine. In 2017, I bought a house there to spend more time with them and expand my worldview. Everyone said it would be good for me. Maui was a perfect place to begin my next chapter, and I took to life there quite easily.

There was a golf course nearby where I could learn the sport for the first time ever, and play a round with newly found friends. I loved to cook and have people over to make pizza or brisket and, of course, my specialty of deli rye bread. Gabby and her family visited often and had a whale of a time in the swimming pool and running down to the beach. I even hired a couple of trainers to come by twice a week to help me get—and stay—fit. It was a great feeling to get a workout in the warm island air, to feel healthy and full of vitality.

From my first days living on Maui, albeit as a part-time resident, I saw tremendous opportunity. I saw a chance to put into practice ideas I'd been learning about and working on for more than fifty years as a committed environmentalist, dating back to my legal work with David Sive and my involvement as a board member of the Natural Resources Defense Council (NRDC).

The NRDC was founded in 1970 by a group including Whitney North Seymour and John Adams—who has been a friend for more than fifty years now—as a way to bring top legal and scientific talent to bear on important environmental issues. Besides Sive, the first NRDC board of directors included a Rockefeller and a Roosevelt, as well as James Marshall and Mrs. Louis S. Auchincloss.

The basic thinking behind environmental work boils down to this: **Don't just think about yourself, think about others and look to the future of the planet, not just your own narrow slice of life. I'd call it the power of kindness elevated to global proportions.**

Maui is a unique and complex place with incredible natural resources, geography, and demographics. To me, given its plentiful sunlight, fertile soil, and clean air, it seemed well-positioned to be completely self-sustaining, with locally grown food, fresh water, and a warm climate, making it easy to provide shelter. As part of the most remote archipelago on earth, the Hawaiian Islands, it's isolated from pollution by adjoining states or countries. Moreover, Hawai'i has a robust history of self-sufficiency pre-Western contact, when over a million Kānaka Maoli (Native Hawaiian people) used a sophisticated land management system to live, farm, and share the land's abundant resources—and be completely self-sufficient.

As I learned about this history and understood the present-day potential, I wondered if it would be possible to create a completely sustainable Maui in every area: food and agriculture, waste disposal, water, energy, transportation, education and employment, and housing. Why don't we try to make Maui a model of sustainability, so that twenty-five, fifty, or even a hundred years from now, people would talk about the Maui Model for sustainability? Something like the Brenton Woods Model in support of the International Monetary

Fund, or the Sweden Model of social spending. I loved the idea. People could apply the "Maui Model" and tweak it to make Minneapolis, Milan, Madrid, or entire countries sustainable.

My first step was to talk to as many people as I could to understand the realities on the ground and generate ideas for possible solutions. I sought out any experts I could find, including anyone working with organizations with similar goals. I remember being a little startled when I spoke about my vision with Tim Bodkin, the head of the Sustainability Living Institute of Maui at the University of Hawai'i Maui College.

"Wow, what a great idea!" he replied.

I couldn't possibly be the first person to suggest the idea, but I did know we had a lot of work to do. I felt energized, and approached the project as I would any business: Let's not try to do something that is already being done well, and let's not reinvent any wheels.

We needed to do a thorough landscape analysis as a precondition of any larger effort. What organizations on the ground were doing work in this area? What was the government doing? What were nonprofits doing? What was going on in each of these individual facets of sustainability? I hired Lily Diamond, a brilliant Yale graduate raised on Maui. Lily spent a year and a half talking to hundreds of supporting organizations and government entities, putting together a detailed and thorough analysis of each of the areas of potential sustainability.

Electric power generation turns out to be one area where progress has been made and bold goals established. Hawai'i earned acclaim by passing a law in 2015 with a goal of achieving 100 percent of its energy through renewables by 2045. The announcement made headlines everywhere from *Scientific American* to Fox News. Barack Obama was President when he tweeted out in June 2015 to his 100 million followers: "Hawai'i just set a goal of generating

100 percent of its electricity from renewable resources." I'd call that making a splash.

Maui County embarked on an even more ambitious trajectory. As the National Renewable Energy Laboratory (NREL) found in a July 2021 article, "Maui is not waiting until 2045 to meet Hawai'i's clean energy mandates: The island is likely to become the first interconnected electric transmission system anywhere to operate with 100 percent wind and solar PV power on an instantaneous basis."

So we concluded that power generation didn't need my help. The more I pored over the results of our study, the more I was able to rule out other areas of work, either because they were already on a good trajectory for sustainability or because I just didn't have the skills or resources to make a real difference any time soon. It was doubtful, for example, that I could make any impact working on large, slow challenges like better road-building and construction of more housing. That would be too much to bite off. It turned out that the area where I felt we could have the best chance of making a real difference would be agriculture, and in particular, food production.

Maui would seem to be well positioned to be self-reliant when it comes to growing its own food. At first glance, you might assume that because food grows so readily—with avocados, bananas, papayas, and mangoes literally falling off the trees in many people's backyards—that the island would provide all or most of the food consumed by its residents.

I was shocked to learn, however, that it's not even close. It turns out that around 90 percent of the food eaten on Maui comes from somewhere else. It's imported and shipped there as air or ocean cargo. People on Maui are so dependent on imports that, at any one time, there is only a four- or five-day supply of food on the island. That means that if the ships and planes stopped coming because of a pandemic, natural disaster, labor strike, or anything else, there would soon be major food shortages on an island of more than 700 square miles, with a population of 160,000 permanent residents and, at any one time, some 300,000 tourists.

That was exactly what happened during a 2012 port strike, and again during the international shortages of the COVID-19 pandemic in 2020. But there are hurdles to local farming, which is always tough, especially on Maui. Land is expensive. Return on investment is minimal. Anything that can be done on behalf of farmers to help grow fresh produce and get it to people more readily seemed worth a deeper look. I soon found out that some smart and committed people were coming up with creative solutions to difficult problems, like Scott Lacasse of the organization Grow Some Good.

Scott is a very inspirational guy. He earned a Masters in Environmental Studies, researching Maui's watersheds and food systems. He joined Grow Some Good in 2019 as a program manager and worked his way up to Executive Director. Scott pitched me on a model of building community farms on available properties, like the YMCA, so that they are near low-income residential areas and might encourage community members to take part in farming and growing food they can eat. The point is: You can't just have a banana diet. (Although, come to think of it, I did have an uncle who went on an all-banana diet. He was diagnosed with cancer at twenty-five and he ate only bananas for a year. He survived the cancer, and lived to be one hundred years old.) And you also can't thrive eating junk food, which is often the only option for communities where fresh produce is scarce, areas dubbed food deserts.

Grow Some Good's hybridized community garden model synthesizes the best practices of traditional allotment gardening with regenerative place-based agroforestry. With Scott's vision and hard work, we decided to direct our efforts and funds to help the organization establish a Community Garden Initiative in a residential area of Kahului, providing local residents with opportunities to grow nourishing, delicious food right in—or near—their backyards. If we are successful, it will not only make a difference in the lives of a few hundred Maui residents, it will provide a model for the rest of the island and hopefully for the country and the world.

My hope is that someday we can end the practice of shipping vast quantities of food across vast distances, and reverse the dependence on mega-farms and mega-farmers. Due to our dependence on these monocropping institutions, soils across the planet have depleted. The world has become dependent on a handful of producers, and left most of us less, rather than more, food secure. Think back to World War II, and the Victory Gardens, when everyone grew what they could to help the war effort by fighting the stateside food shortage. An estimated 20 million people joined in then, planting gardens in empty lots, city rooftops, or their own backyards.

The more we can connect communities to their local farmers and give them options aside from purchasing goods shipped in from thousands of miles away, the more we'll begin to change people's mindsets. Not to mention it's much healthier to eat locally grown foods.

I hope that the Maui Community Garden Initiative will provide a model—across the state, the country, and maybe even across the world—for increasing not just the production, but also the consumption, of locally grown food. Hopefully, the initiative will demonstrate that nourishing crops can be grown where people actually live and that those people will want to consume *that* produce rather than shop for imported food. If we accomplish that goal, we will have gone a long way toward caring for our planet, protecting our resources, and addressing the challenges of systemic inequality.

In the process of analyzing what was already being done to advance food sustainability, I met many inspiring and passionate people. These are people who, if they realize their dreams, will make big dents in the quest toward food sustainability. Scott Lacasse is one of them. Bobby Pahia, and his daughter, Kiana Reyes, are two others. Bobby's ancestors farmed kalo (taro) for generations in Hawai'i, and his work today is to innovate that field—to prove, in fact, that regenerative farming is feasible as a method that is not only kind to the earth and our human family, but is also economically lucrative.

Based on 310 acres in Waikapu that was monocropped with sugarcane for over a century, Pahia now manages a number of other farmers who sublease the land to grow a diversity of crops, native Hawaiian plants, and livestock—all of which serve to restore the parched soil and move towards Pahia's goals of feeding the community. In 2022, Reyes founded Kanu Aloha Community Farm on 2.5 acres of that land, a project sponsored in part by our grant to Grow Some Good. Together, this family is changing how Maui eats.

Jennifer Karaca, Founding Executive Director of Common Ground Collective, is another community member innovating for good. Jennifer has a fascinating background. She's from the Midwest, but served in the U.S. Army and has taught in Costa Rica, Peru, and Turkey. She studied Sustainable Science Management at the University of Hawai'i campus on Maui, which is one of the foremost sustainability programs in the country. She was so inspired by her studies there that she came up with a novel idea: to seek out homeowners who had a little bit of land, anywhere from half an acre to several acres, which might lie fallow or be undeveloped. Once she could find homeowners with land willing to join the program, she could then pair them with farmers who needed land to farm.

It was a wonderful pitch: "Look, your land will be attentively cultivated, and whatever is grown, you can have as much of it as you want. If we sell the produce, then we'll share a portion of the proceeds with you, or you can direct us to give it away to the needy."

The idea was brilliant for solving the basic problem of potential farmland being way too expensive on Maui. Too often, the numbers just didn't add up for aspiring farmers: They could work ten lifetimes farming the land and never come close to the profit someone might make using that same land for real estate or other development purposes.

Karaca had an excellent idea, but unfortunately not great timing. She went to work signing up farmers and homeowners to join her program and made quick progress. In fact, she had more than a hundred land owners ready to share their land when the pandemic hit and derailed her efforts.

She knew she had to bide her time with that program, but in the meantime, she came up with a way to get Common Ground Collective started: She went to the landowners she had signed on to her farming program and offered to harvest produce growing on trees that were already on their land, which would otherwise go to waste. You see it all over: Avocados, for example, grow like dandelions on Maui. In many areas of the island, it's common to see ripe avocados falling off trees and rotting on the ground. Same with mangoes, bananas, citrus, and other fruit.

"Let us pick your produce," Jennifer told homeowners. "We'll sell it to a merchant or at a farmer's market, and share the proceeds. Everyone comes out ahead."

The first year, Jennifer personally picked 4,000 pounds. Last year, she and one associate picked more than 45,000 pounds of fruit that would have otherwise been wasted, and sold that. Their efforts demonstrated that it was possible to achieve a strong social good with a little bit of ingenuity, and a lot of effort.

Vincent Mina, the former head of the local farmer's union, Hawai'i Farmers Union United, is another hero. Vincent used to be a house painter. He has what he calls the smallest farm in the world, just 2,500 square feet, the size of a small house, everything included. It's quite ingeniously conceived and executed. He harvests hundreds of pounds of sprouts each week, all organic, of course, and sells them for $15 a pound to all the fancy local hotels and restaurants on Maui. He has an automated sprinkler system that he designed and built with white PVC, and a humidifier with a detector, so when it's not humid enough, it sprays water.

Vincent built this whole thing himself. He has an array of seven tables, each not much bigger than a normal dinner table, all of them loaded with trays. First he soaks the seeds—alfalfa, bean, mustard, and pea seeds, everything you'd want in a salad. The sprouts grow and after seven days are harvested. Then he takes the roots and whatever else is left and puts that in a covered half-drum, along with scrap boxes from Amazon that he chops up, and composts the mixture, with the help of a robust population of earth-worms. He takes that freshly composted soil and uses it for a fresh batch of sprouts. Vincent has demonstrated that you can grow tons—literally tons—of nourishing produce on a tiny plot of land.

Another innovator for food sustainability is John Dobovan of Kulahaven Farms. John set up an elaborate "closed-circuit" system to grow both produce and fish in Kula, 3,500 feet high on the slopes of Haleakalā, near the weekly farmer's market I like to visit. Another graduate of the University of Hawai'i Maui College program in Sustainable Tropical Crop Management, John is part of a movement that gives me hope for the Maui Model. At Kula-haven, John farmed raised beds of watercress alongside twelve large tanks—each home to different-aged rainbow trout, varying from newly fertilized eggs to two-pound fish. Each month, he took out the two-pounders, which were ready to be sold to restaurants on island, and put in one-inchers, which take about a year to reach two pounds. The water flowed through the fish tanks and into the raised beds, where the waste products functioned as fertilizer, a glorious perpetual motion machine yielding both watercress and top-quality farmed trout. Though Kulahaven Farm closed its doors this year, John's model remains inspirational.

Though all of these initiatives—and no doubt thousands of others like them across the world—are long shots, I am optimistic and energized by the commitment and passion of people like Scott Lacasse, Bobby Pahia, Kiana Reyes, Jennifer Karaca, Vincent Mina, and John Dobovan. As Margaret Mead, the famous anthropologist, said: "Never doubt that a small group of thoughtful, committed citizens can change the world. Indeed, it is the only thing that ever has."

CHAPTER 22

The True Measure of Success (and Oh, Don't Bluff Willie Nelson)

As a young professional embarking on my career, I looked up to entrepreneurs who made a splash when they were young, noticing opportunities nobody else did—figures like Walmart's Sam Walton or FedEx's Fred Smith, and today's Bill Gates or Mark Zuckerberg. These were people who came up with big ideas in their twenties and made a lot of money early on—but their focus wasn't on kindness. Now, at 82, the way I measure success looks different. **Sure, one component of success is about entrepreneurship and wealth, but true success, I believe, is about making a difference in the world through kindness.** And while financial abundance is a helpful tool in the process of making change at a community or global scale, it's just one part of the picture. True success isn't measured by numbers in a bank account or on a stock exchange ticker. It's measured by real-life change in the way people live and the way they help others to live.

These days, my idols are men and women whose ambition is focused on making important, relevant contributions to society— well into their eighties and nineties. It's this kind of vision and action that I want to embody, so I began to look for examples of it within my own communities: People who are successful *and* kind. People who are willing to put themselves on the line to make a positive change in the world. People who make a difference. People like Willie Nelson.

Willie might have been born in Texas and lived in Nashville for years, but by the time I bought my home on Maui, he'd been an island fixture for decades. Willie raised some of his kids on Maui, was a beloved part of the community, and—second only to his music and his philanthropy—was known for his legendary poker game. Artists even painted pictures of Willie's games! Charlie's, once the main eatery and drinking hole in the historic town of Pā'ia, had a massive oil painting of the scene. If you stopped into a souvenir shop, you'd literally see prints and paintings of Willie at his card table with a wild crew of characters—actors like Woody Harrelson and Owen Wilson, and former NBA coach Don Nelson, all Maui regulars.

I admire Willie for many reasons. He champions progressive causes and social justice—from co-founding Farm Aid to support family farmers to advocating for Native American rights and environmental causes. Willie has an instinct for doing what's right, at the right time. He is an advocate for kindness, and demonstrates that in everything he does publicly and privately.

It's no surprise then that one of my goals when I bought my home on Maui was to play some poker with Willie. The games are known to be great fun, with a lot of lively back and forth, and rough humor. Woody Harrelson once went on *Jimmy Kimmel Live* and explained that he'd lost so much in the card games, "I've built a wing on Willie's house."

Don Nelson confirmed that: "Woody makes me laugh, but Woody is not a good card player," he said. "He'll lose the whole farm. Owen Wilson is a pretty good player. He doesn't lose much."

Sure, I wanted to see what all the fuss was about. But I also wanted to connect with people like Willie and Don—people who exuded kindness, who became massively successful in tough, often dog-eat-dog professions, while remaining unapologetically kind—and understand how they'd continued to find meaning and purpose in the later years of their lives. I wanted to share their karma. The fact that all this was riding on getting into a poker game became a kind of joke with my daughter, Gabby.

"I've got to get into Willie's card game!" I'd tell her with mock seriousness.

"I'm sure you will, Dad," she'd say indulgently.

For me it was a fun little challenge, wondering how one might go about getting invited into a legendary, private card game. I would ask people I met on Maui if they had ever played in Willie Nelson's poker game. Some of them had never even played cards, let alone with Willie—but finally I found one person who had, and had found the clouds of cannabis smoke a little disorienting.

"I played one hand," he told me. "I lost $1,000 on that first hand and got up and left."

The singer Jack Johnson joined the game, and in 2015 wrote a song, "Willie Got Me Stoned and Stole All of My Money," which he performed at Farm Aid 2015 in Saratoga Springs, New York.

Here are the first few lines:

Willie got me stoned and took all my money
I was fifty dollars up and then my mind went funny
It didn't really help that I didn't know the rules of the game
And it probably didn't help that I couldn't remember my name

Later, it continues:

After Willie got me stoned, took me for everything I had

I had to walk home, I had no money for a cab
I didn't have the heart to ask anybody for a ride
And nobody in the room looked in a condition to drive

I was up for the challenge, I thought, if given a chance. I'm a fair card player myself. But years passed with no progress on my good-natured campaign to get into the game. Then one day I found out that my trainers, Brian and Chris Mercer, also trained Willie. That happened to be around the time I was planning my eightieth birthday celebration, and I figured if you couldn't ask then, when would be the time?

"Brian," I said, more in jest than not, "next time you're working with Willie, could you ask him if he'd come and play at my birthday?"

They passed on the message and sure enough, the next Tuesday, Brian had encouraging news. "I talked to Annie, Willie's wife," he told me. "You should email Willie's agent in New York, and see what he can do."

Now, obviously, I didn't expect Willie to come sing at my birthday party. I was just trying to get the ball rolling.

I put my all into that email to Mark Rothbaum, Willie's manager, in New York. I crafted a masterpiece of an email, an email that would bring tears to your eyes it was so good. Willie and I were compatriots, fellow octogenarians who hold the same values. I mentioned everyone and everything that might show a connection to Willie. I paused a moment before I actually hit SEND on the email, excited to be firing this one off into the void.

Then I sent the email—and almost instantly received a reply. Truly, it was bizarre. Within seconds, my inbox showed an email reply from Rothbaum. It was not a reply I enjoyed reading.

"Happy future birthday Sig," he wrote back. "Willie won't be attending your celebration but does wish you to know eighty is nothing, a mere number. All the best."

That Friday, on my trainers' next regular visit, Brian and Chris excitedly asked if I'd heard back from the agent. I said I had.

"What did he say?" Brian wanted to know.

"Well I don't have my phone on me to show you," I answered, "but basically he said, 'Fuck you, happy birthday.'"

Brian was horrified, and said I had to let them talk to Willie's wife again. One day later, Brian emailed me:

"Aloha Sig! So Monday night Willie has invited you to play poker. It's just an invite for you because they are limiting Django's (his poker room) to just five people right now, due to the pandemic. Give me a call when you have some free time and I'll fill you in."

I was thrilled! Elated! And knew I had some serious training to do. I'd have to practice puffing on a joint without coughing if I was going to show up for Willie's card game. In my entire life I'd smoked marijuana only a few dozen times; my lifetime consumption might have added up to less than what Willie, famous for his tolerance, used to consume in one day. When even Snoop Dogg says Willie Nelson smoked him under the table, that's saying something.

I called up Gabby, who was coming over the next day.

"You have to do me a favor," I told her.

"Sure Dad, what?"

"Can you bring along a joint? I need to practice."

"No problem," she said.

I was all but pacing the next day, waiting for Gabby to arrive. Every time in recent years I'd taken a puff on a joint, or even tried a vape pen, I coughed. Sometimes I coughed a lot. I assumed I must be doing something wrong, like the Pinto character in *Animal House*. (The professor played by Donald Sutherland encourages him, "Try not to drool quite so much.") I needed to work on my technique.

Finally Gabby and her family arrived. The kids splashed around in the pool for a while, then went down to the beach—and at last, it was 8:30 p.m. and they went upstairs to play and get ready for bed. It was my chance to pull my daughter aside.

"Ok, Gabby," I said, rubbing my hands together with anticipation. "Let's try it!"

She gave me a blank stare.

"Try what?" she asked.

"The joint!"

"Oh my god," she covered her face with her hands. "I forgot it!"

I had one day before my card game at Willie's, and I'd been banking on a little practice with Gabby. No dice! I tried puffing through a straw, but that was useless. Air didn't make me cough, smoke did.

At least I felt comfortable about my card-playing. I'd been playing poker since I was a five-year-old kid in New York City. My mother taught me how to play, using pennies for bets, and I developed my own style, as Gabby reminded me.

"Everyone talks about a good poker face, but the more that you psychologically understand your opponent, the more of an edge that gives you," she said as we talked that night. "So I'm sure in poker, kindness could also be a good strategy."

That's me. It's how I play the game—competitive, but kind to a fault.

"Just play that strategy where you're super honest," Gabby encouraged me.

She was right. I would often start out a hand by telling the truth. "Look," I'd say. "I just want to tell you guys that I have an extraordinary hand. So if you don't want to lose your money, I would say fold your cards now. Otherwise, stay in. But I have a very, very good hand." And in the end, I'd show my cards and I might have a straight or another very good hand. But sometimes, just often enough to keep everyone on edge, I'd be bluffing.

Monday evening arrived and I showed up at Willie's house right at 6:30. Annie walked me out to a little room set up for poker next to his garage, Django's. Clearly the man had played a lot of poker in that room. It had a lived-in look, comfortable and inviting. There were mementos here and there, including a platinum record, a bottle or two of bourbon and some good bottles of wine, along with soda and other drinks. Someone brought sandwiches. There was even a bowl of guacamole. It was all very welcoming.

I walked in and sat down next to Don Nelson, who everyone calls Nellie, the former Boston Celtics player and coach of the Golden State Warriors and Dallas Mavericks. Willie flashed me a warm smile, greeted me, and wished me a happy birthday. His kindness shone through in the first seconds of meeting. Willie was eighty-eight, but full of energy and presence—there was nothing old about the way he acted.

And he was ready to get to the game. "Okay, the buy-in is $300," he said, all business, and we dealt some cards. A few other guys joined us and added to the conviviality—and the pot.

Willie's games are famous for a number of things, starting with the colorful characters, and moving on to the highly creative variations on straight poker they cook up at the table. I had been playing poker for seventy-five years at that point, but they were playing games I couldn't even understand: "Sprecklesville," "Oldtimers," "Nines are wild," and "Dirty Nellie," where your low hole card is wild. Nellie himself was kind enough to help me get up to speed.

"What is this crazy game?" I'd ask him, and he'd laugh and explain it again.

Ten minutes into the game came my moment of truth. Willie pulled out an electric vape pen and sucked long and hard on it, exhaling magnificently. We all watched with proper appreciation. Then he leaned over, past Nellie, to offer it to me.

"Sig?" he asked courteously.

I'm used to quick decisions, but my mind was racing. On the one hand, I was thinking: *Shit, if I take a puff and start coughing here, these six guys are going to throw me out! It's Covid time and they're not going to want me around! And the pen just came out of Willie's mouth. What if he has Covid?* That was one side of me. Another side implored a new way of thinking: *I've been waiting years to spend some time with Willie. How often in my life am I going to have a chance to play poker and smoke a joint with Willie Nelson, directly from his lips to mine? C'mon, live a little!* Back and forth, the two sides of my brain went at it.

"Sure!" I offered brightly.

I took a little puff and inhaled. Amazingly, I didn't cough. Not even a little bit. What a relief! I got a little high, enough to feel good but not enough to cloud my mind. And what a night it was. I had a blast. Willie is a very good card player, aggressive, sharp, exceedingly nice, and truly great company; we all felt lucky to sit around that table and soak up the vibe.

Once I got through my worries about coughing, I was totally relaxed and played my cards that way, not worried about anything, not trying to press my advantage when I had it, just going with the luck of the deal. And guess what? I went on a hot streak. Good hand after good hand. I was the big winner of the night—a real surprise! Willie just about broke even, if my recollection is right.

I have since played many times at Willie's place, and when he's not around, at Nellie's poker room. They became my friends, and I relish the time I spend with them.

At age ninety, Willie is still touring, and I was happy to show up at the Shoreline Amphitheatre in Mountain View, California—home of Google—to see him perform as part of the Outlaw Music Festival in October 2022. I even got a chance to meet briefly with Willie and Annie just before Willie and his son Micah performed.

"Hi Sig!" Annie called out brightly. "No poker tonight!" Willie might have slowed down a little, but he was still very much Willie, an utter original with a big heart.

Getting to know Willie and Don offered me a template for what the next decade of my own life might look like. Not only have they had legendary careers, but they also continue to impact the world with acts of lovingkindness every day. They are active, relevant, and caring at a time in their lives when most of their peers are retired. It's this energy—of curiosity, of possibility, of a commitment to making a difference—that inspires me every day.

Kindness in Action

This book marks the beginning of a new effort called the Kindness Initiative, to honor and celebrate kindness among young school-children. I am hopeful we can start a revolution in which the next generation of children feel so good about caring for others that they radiate kindness in their families and communities, drowning out the din of cruelty that a small handful of people create. Like a business, we will start small, create a working model at a partner school, learn from challenges that arise in implementation, refine the Initiative through feedback, and figure out how to scale it throughout the country—and hopefully the world.

To recognize and honor the power of kindness for people in their most impressionable years, we plan to sponsor Kindness Projects and give out monthly It Pays To Be Kind awards in middle schools across the country. We have a perfect test site on Maui, where my friend Mike Rose, a former educator voted best middle school teacher on Maui five years in a row, is developing the pilot program with a group of exceptional teachers in the community. If the pilot works as we expect, I hope to expand our efforts across the country.

While the Kindness Projects will provide kids with a tangible and interactive way to embody kindness and spread acts of kindness within their schools and among their peers, the Awards will celebrate kindness as a powerful life force, recognizing schoolchildren and young adults who demonstrate kindness through their words and actions. Both the Projects and the Awards ceremonies will inspire people of all ages to extend kindness throughout their communities, person by person, smile by smile. Before long, if all goes as planned, we hope to turn this into a national—and international—movement. As the project grows, the Awards will also recognize public figures for being exemplars of kindness in the world.

Would you like to be an ambassador of kindness, or are you part of a school or community group that can help us spread the word? Visit *kindnesspays.org* to learn more.

The Startup Formula for Success

The Basic Startup Formula

1.

FLESH OUT THE VISION

2.

TALK TO A LOT OF PEOPLE WHO KNOW
WHAT THEY'RE DOING

3.

FIGURE OUT WHAT HAS TO BE DONE
AND WHAT HUMAN AND CASH RESOURCES
YOU NEED TO DO IT

4.

WRITE UP A PLAN OF ACTION

5.

GET TO WORK

6.

AND NEVER GIVE UP

(Page 99)

Sig's Tips for Startup Success

1. **BE KIND**
   Being a little kind goes a long way. (p. 2, 12)

2. **LISTEN**
   Learn how to listen to people. (p. 22)

3. **LEARN FROM THE EXPERTS**
   You don't have to be an expert in everything to become a good leader, but you do have to be willing to study and learn from the experts along the way. (p. 28)

4. **BE CURIOUS**
   Look at a business or difficult situation with an open mind and ask as many questions as you need to until you can understand what's getting in the way of it working optimally. (pp. 66, 94)

5. **INNOVATE**
   For a startup to work, an idea needs to be ahead of its time, but not too far ahead. (pp. 94, 95, 128)

6. **INSPIRE PEOPLE WITH YOUR VISION**
   Motivate others—employees, investors, friends, and family—to share your vision by passionately enrolling them in your dreams. (p. 137)

7. **BE CONFIDENT**

    Investors invest in people, not ideas. They put their faith in people they think are smart, honest, and determined. (p. 112)

8. **LEARN FROM FAILURE**

    Failure is part of the process of maturing in business, and most employers and investors ascribe value to the experience. (p. 92)

9. **KEEP GOING**

    Instead of giving up in your darkest moments, sit down, re-center, and think about what your next startup could be. (pp. 48, 89)

10. **BE COURAGEOUS**

    Always ask the hard questions, especially from investors, even if you might not like the answers. (p. 106)

11. **BE WILLING TO COURSE CORRECT**

    Use trial and error to evolve: Track progress. Understand what's working and what's not. Keep tweaking the product until you get it right. (p. 104)

12. **KNOW WHEN TO LET GO**

    Nurture the winning ideas and don't waste time on what's not working. (p. 106)

13. **KNOW YOUR LIMITS AND HAVE PATIENCE**

    Don't expand before you're ready. More companies die of indigestion—growing too fast—than from starvation. (p. 105)

14. BE OPTIMISTIC

Stay away from naysayers and surround yourself with optimists. Align with people with a can-do attitude, no matter what their background. (p. 111)

15. PASSION OVER EXPERTISE

Sometimes expertise and industry experience lead to learning bad habits and blinding yourself. Blank slates who are on board with your vision can be helpful as first hires. (pp. 111, 112)

16. BUILD AN A-TEAM

Develop an A-Team of leaders. Hire smart, talented players with good synergy and get them to work together—they don't individually have to be perfect, but together they create the A-Team. (pp. 137, 138)

17. EXPECT GREATNESS

You can be demanding but also kind, serious but also seriously committed to having good relationships. Make it clear that there's no room for phoning it in, cutting corners, or misleading anyone. (pp. 31, 173)

18. BE HUMBLE

Understand you don't have to be the smartest person in the room, just the person who knows how to align yourself with the people who can make your vision a reality. (p. 101)

19. ACCEPT HELP

Don't always try to reinvent the wheel. If you don't need to build it yourself, and can buy or rent it, then do that. (p. 169)

20. PAY ATTENTION TO CONNECTION

Pay attention to the people that you meet, they just might change your life down the road. (p. 109)

21. CULTIVATE COMPASSION

The people that you work with are your family, treat them that way. (pp. 41, 127)

22. TRUST PEOPLE TO DO THEIR JOB

Trust your leadership team and keep your fingers out of everyone else's pie. (p. 138)

23. PERSEVERE

Be prepared to overcome setbacks and mistakes. (p. 132)

24. BE HONEST

Cultivating a company culture of honesty and transparency supports everyone, and makes space for positive change in the world. (pp. 140, 141, 163)

25. ACT IN INTEGRITY

There's always a way to act in kindness, even when the circumstances may be unpleasant or challenging. (pp. 135, 140)

26. MAKE A DIFFERENCE

A true measure of a person's success is their contribution to the world. (p. 178, 187)

ACKNOWLEDGMENTS

I'm grateful to my parents, Rose and Simon Anderman, for instilling in me the values that helped me thrive, and to my sisters, Pearl Ratushewitz and Carol Harkavy, for being my forever cheerleaders. Thanks to my children Elissa Van Deursen, David Anderman, and Gabby Anderman—and my grandchildren—for keeping me young and on my toes. Thank you to my wife, Jo Anderman, for her buoyant love and support. Tremendous gratitude to my business associates, especially Limin Hu and Jonathan Corr, who were instrumental in making Ellie Mae a success—and to Barr Dolan, who made the first investment in Ellie Mae and had blind faith in my ability to pull it off. Many thanks to the team of teachers helping to birth the Kindness Initiative in schools around the country. And to the team who made this book a reality: Steve Kettmann for his encouragement and help in conceiving and writing the book; Lily Diamond for editorial wizardry; Heather Scott for design genius; Stefani Milan for publishing coordination.

And of course, to Susan.

ABOUT THE AUTHOR

Sig Anderman is a businessman, attorney, and philanthropist whose life's work has been infused with kindness—both practicing it and receiving it. He was born in New York City and attended New York public schools until he earned a Bachelor of Laws degree from New York University. Sig's career spans historic casework in environmental law alongside industry forefather David Sive and pioneering entrepreneurship as the CEO of four real estate technology companies, including American Home Shield (NASDAQ: FTDR) and Ellie Mae (NYSE: ELLI), which was acquired for over $11 billion. As founder of the Springboard Initiative and the Kindness Initiative, and director of the Anderman Family Foundation, Sig's legacy of kindness expresses itself through educational, environmental, and social justice efforts nationwide.

A NOTE ABOUT THE TYPE

This book was set in Adobe Caslon. William Caslon released his first typefaces in 1722. Caslon's types were based on seventeenth-century Dutch old style designs, which were then used extensively in England. Because of their remarkable practicality, Caslon's types became popular throughout Europe and the American colonies; printer Benjamin Franklin hardly used any other typeface. The first printings of the American Declaration of Independence and the Constitution were set in Caslon. For her Caslon revival, designer Carol Twombly studied specimen pages printed by William Caslon between 1734 and 1770.

LEARN MORE

www.kindnesspays.org